THE 300 GREATEST FOOTBALL FEATS

Copyright © 2024 Smart People

All rights reserved.

ISBN: 9798323283705

Summary

Introduction 5

Football: The Origins of a Global Passion 7

The Greatest Exploits in English Football History 8

World records in football 10

Technical Prowess in Women's Football 16

Historic Performances by Players 18

Technological Advancements 21

Moments of Technical Brilliance 22

Technical and Tactical Innovations in Football 24

Career Pinnacles of Individual Players 26

Did You Know? 28

Undefeated Records 30

Amazing anecdotes 32

Match Turnarounds 34

Fair Play and Acts of Great Class 36

Legendary Performances in Finals 38

Exceptional Tournament Performances 40

Decisive Victories Under Pressure 42

Young Talent Prowess 44

Singular Moments of Brilliance 46

Tactical Masterworks of Coaches 49

Unexpected Successes of Underestimated Teams 50
Astonishing Football Facts 52
The Most Beautiful Goal Celebrations in Football History .. 54
Memorable Technical Feats in Football................................... 56
Well-Kept Secrets 58
Humanitarian and Charitable Impact of Football Stars 60
Speed Records on the Field... 63
Outstanding Goalkeeper Performances................................. 64
Achievements of Disabled Players 66
Achievements in Derbies and Rivalries 68
Transfer Records and Economic Impacts 71
Apex of Historic Clubs 72
Crushing Victories and Match Dominations 74
Triumphant Injury Comebacks 76
Record Attendances and Extraordinary Atmospheres 78
Football in Unusual Places..80
Success and Progress in Women's football 82
What Kind of Football Player Are You?................................. 84
QUIZ 86
Introduction to Euro 2024 90
Euro 2024 Predictions... 96

Introduction

Welcome to an extraordinary journey into the heart of football, a sport that captivates millions of hearts around the world. This book is not just a compilation; it is a celebration of the moments that have defined football, a tribute to the feats that have marked its history, and a dive into the anecdotes that bring this game to life.

Whether you are a young enthusiast discovering the joys of the beautiful game or an adult who has followed many seasons, this book offers you a unique window into the feats that have shaped this sport. Each page transports you to a world where courage, talent, and determination meet to create unforgettable moments.

Through these 300 exploits, you will relive spectacular goals, breathtaking technical maneuvers, unlikely turnarounds, and stories of team spirit and perseverance that illustrate why football is so beloved.

But this book goes beyond mere facts and figures. The anecdotes, little-known facts, and unveiled secrets offer a more intimate and personal perspective of football. You will discover stories that show the human dimension of the sport, revealing the emotions, dreams, and challenges of football icons.

Moreover, we have included a personality test. Find out what type of football player you would be, which legend inspires you the most.

This book is your passport to experiencing and reliving the magic of football, to understanding its nuances, and to celebrating its victories. Each page brings you closer to the essence of football, inviting you to share in the excitement, passion, and inspiration that emanate from this universal game.

Prepare to be transported into the most exhilarating moments of football, to explore its hidden facets, and to celebrate the sport that unites the world. Embark on this football adventure and let the spirit of the game illuminate your passion for football.

In addition to covering historical events and unforgettable moments of global football, a special part of this book is dedicated to Euro 2024. This section offers a deep dive into the tournament, highlighting the teams, matches, and players who will define this eagerly awaited competition.

And to further enrich your experience, note that this book is presented entirely in color. Each page is a visual window that allows you to plunge into the intensity and brilliance of football.

This deliberate choice to use color is not merely aesthetic; it reflects the vibrancy and dynamics of football, a sport where every color carries an emotion, a story, an identity.

Football: The Origins of a Global Passion

Football, the Universal Sport

Football is undoubtedly the most popular sport in the world. Played in every country by hundreds of millions of people of all ages, it stirs passions and generates unparalleled enthusiasm. But where did this king of sports come from? What are its origins, and how did it conquer the entire planet? Let us dive into the fascinating history of this game that thrills crowds.

The Ancient Roots of the Beautiful Game

While modern football was born in the 19th century in England, its roots trace back to antiquity. As early as the 3rd century BC, the Chinese played a game called "cuju," which involved kicking a leather ball filled with feathers into a net using their feet. In ancient Greece, "episkyros" pitted two teams against each other with the goal of carrying a ball beyond the opponent's goal line. The Romans played "harpastum," a mix of football and rugby.

During the Middle Ages, ball games involving entire villages were popular in France and England. However, their violence led authorities to ban them several times. It was ultimately in the English schools of the 19th century that football began to be codified. The first written rule prohibiting the handling of the ball with hands dates from 1823.

The Birth of Modern Football in England

The foundational act of modern football was the establishment of the Football Association in England in 1863, which set the first official rules. The field had to be rectangular, the ball spherical, and carrying it with the hands was forbidden. Quickly, football became structured with the creation of the English Cup in 1871, professionalism in 1885, and the championship in 1888.

The success was immediate, and football spread like wildfire throughout the rest of the United Kingdom and then to continental Europe and South America via British workers and engineers. Clubs were formed everywhere, and national competitions emerged. In 1904, FIFA (International Federation of Association Football) was established in Paris to harmonize the rules globally. Football became a universal sport.

A Simple and Spectacular Game

The genius of football lies in the simplicity of its rules. Two teams of 11 players each compete with the objective of sending a round ball into the opponent's goal, using any part of their body except their arms and hands, except for the goalkeeper within his penalty area. A match lasts 90 minutes, divided into two halves of 45 minutes.

But behind this apparent simplicity lies a deep subtlety. Football is a highly tactical and spectacular game. Players must demonstrate technique, creativity, and quick thinking to dribble, pass, and shoot. The collective dimension is crucial, with a clever balance between offense and defense, short passes, and long balls. Each action can lead to spectacular feats that ignite the stands.

Football, a Mirror of Our Societies

More than just a sport, football is a true societal phenomenon. By its global popularity, it reflects the changes in our world. Professionalization, economic globalization, political issues, and the fight against racism: all major themes permeate the world of football.

Football also conveys strong values: team spirit, respect, tolerance, and solidarity. It brings people together across differences. Whether rich or poor, regardless of skin color, religion, or nationality, everyone can kick a ball. Football is a powerful tool for social integration and empowerment.

A Passion Beyond the Stadium

Football is not limited to 22 players on a field. It also includes the public that lives the matches intensely, from the smallest amateur division to the World Cup. Stadiums are places of communion where joy, fervor, and sometimes disillusionment are expressed. Tifos, chants, and animations in the stands are an integral part of the spectacle.

This passion extends beyond sports venues. In the streets, at the office, in schools, football is an inexhaustible topic of conversation that creates social bonds. Team jerseys, video games, sports betting: football has become a colossal market generating billions of dollars.

The Grand International Tournaments, the Pinnacle of Football Emotion

The apex of football occurs every four years at the World Cup. Established in 1930, it brings together the best nations of the planet in a competition watched by billions. Winning this trophy is the ultimate dream of every player and triggers immense fervor in the winning country.

On a continental level, competitions such as the Euro, Copa America, and the Africa Cup of Nations also generate great fervor. Matches between nations take on a dimension that goes beyond the sporting framework. The national team becomes the standard-bearer of a country, sparking passion and unity around the jersey.

To experience the most thrilling actions, scan the QR code located at the end of the book.

The Greatest Exploits in English Football History

English football has witnessed numerous remarkable achievements throughout its rich history. From World Cup triumphs to record-breaking individual performances, the exploits of English football's finest have left an indelible mark on the sport. In this article, we will delve into ten of the most extraordinary accomplishments that have shaped the landscape of English football and captivated fans across generations.

1. Alan Shearer, the Premier League's All-Time Top Scorer

Alan Shearer's incredible goal-scoring prowess saw him net a record-breaking 260 goals in the Premier League. He scored 112 times for Blackburn Rovers, helping them win the title in 1995, before adding 148 more goals for his beloved Newcastle United. Shearer's predatory instincts in the box earned him the Premier League Golden Boot on three occasions, cementing his status as one of the greatest strikers in English football history. His consistency, power, and clinical finishing made him a defender's nightmare and a fan favorite throughout his illustrious career.

2. England's Triumph on Home Soil: 1966 World Cup Victory

England's greatest footballing triumph came on home soil in 1966 when they won their first and only World Cup. In a thrilling final at Wembley Stadium, the Three Lions overcame West Germany 4-2 after extra time. The match is remembered for Geoff Hurst's hat-trick, the first and only one scored in a World Cup final. Hurst's controversial second goal, which bounced down off the crossbar, has been debated for decades. The victory sparked wild celebrations across the country and remains the pinnacle of England's footballing achievements.

3. Frank Lampard: The Midfield Maestro

Frank Lampard's remarkable consistency and scoring ability from midfield saw him notch 177 Premier League goals during his spells at West Ham United, Chelsea, and Manchester City. This feat is a record for a midfielder in the English top-flight. Lampard's professionalism, work ethic, and technical ability made him a complete player and a key figure in Chelsea's success. He won three Premier League titles and the Champions League with the Blues, cementing his place as one of the greatest midfielders in Premier League history.

4. Michael Owen's Unforgettable 2001

2001 was a year to remember for Michael Owen and Liverpool. The young striker's scintillating form helped the Reds win a historic treble, lifting the FA Cup, League Cup, and UEFA Cup. Owen's speed, movement, and finishing ability terrorized defenses all season long. His performances were recognized with the prestigious Ballon d'Or award, making him the first English winner since Kevin Keegan in 1979. Owen's success in 2001 marked the high point of his career and a golden era for Liverpool Football Club.

5. Manchester United's Treble-Winning Season

In 1999, Manchester United made history by becoming the first English club to win the Premier League, FA Cup, and Champions League in the same season. Under the guidance of Sir Alex Ferguson, the Red Devils showcased their never-say-die attitude, scoring dramatic late goals in each competition. The crowning moment came in the Champions League final against Bayern Munich when substitutes Teddy Sheringham and Ole Gunnar Solskjaer scored in injury time to secure a stunning 2-1 victory. This incredible achievement cemented United's status as one of the greatest clubs in world football.

6. Wayne Rooney: England's All-Time Leading Scorer

Wayne Rooney's 53 goals for England saw him become the country's all-time leading scorer in 2017, surpassing the long-standing record held by Sir Bobby Charlton. Rooney's international career spanned 13 years and 119 appearances, showcasing his longevity and importance to the national team. His combination of skill, strength, and passion made him a talismanic figure for the Three Lions. Rooney's record-breaking goal came from the penalty spot against Switzerland, a fitting way for the striker to write his name into the history books.

7. Arsenal's Dramatic 1979 FA Cup Final Comeback

Arsenal's victory in the 1979 FA Cup final is one of the most dramatic in the competition's history. Trailing 2-0 to Manchester United with just five minutes remaining, the Gunners looked down and out. However, a quick-fire double from Alan Sunderland and Brian Talbot leveled the scores, forcing extra time. In the 89th minute, Sunderland latched onto a cross from Liam Brady to score the winner, sending Arsenal fans into raptures. This incredible comeback showcased the Gunners' fighting spirit and remains one of the club's most iconic moments.

8. Chelsea's Double Delight Under Ancelotti

In the 2009-2010 season, Chelsea achieved a historic Premier League and FA Cup double under the management of Carlo Ancelotti. The Blues were a force to be reckoned with, losing just six games all season. Didier Drogba was the star of the show, scoring 37 goals in all competitions, including the winner in the FA Cup final against Portsmouth. Chelsea's free-flowing, attacking football was a joy to watch, with the likes of Frank Lampard, Florent Malouda, and Nicolas Anelka all playing key roles in the team's success.

9. Arsenal's Invincible Season

The 2003-2004 Premier League season saw Arsenal achieve the unprecedented feat of going unbeaten throughout the entire campaign. Arsène Wenger's side, nicknamed "The Invincibles," won 26 games and drew 12, becoming the first team in the modern era to avoid defeat in a 38-game season. Thierry Henry was the talisman, scoring 30 league goals, while Patrick Vieira, Robert Pires, and Dennis Bergkamp provided the creative spark. The Gunners' blend of skill, speed, and resilience made them an unstoppable force, and their unbeaten record remains one of the greatest achievements in English football history.

10. David Beckham's Last-Gasp Free Kick Rescues England

In October 2001, David Beckham produced a moment of magic to secure England's qualification for the 2002 World Cup. With the Three Lions trailing Greece 2-1 and facing the prospect of a playoff, Beckham stepped up in the dying seconds to score a stunning free kick from 30 yards out. The ball curled over the wall and into the top corner, sending the Old Trafford crowd into delirium. Beckham's goal salvaged a 2-2 draw and ensured England's place at the World Cup, cementing his status as a national hero.

World records in football

These feats are not just numbers in the annals of sports; they represent moments of grace, perseverance, and unmatched excellence. From individual agility to collective triumphs, each record tells a story of determination and passion. Discover the players and teams who have made history by setting new standards of excellence, leaving an indelible mark on the world of football.

1. AS Roma, the Longest Winning Streak in Serie A

During the 2013-2014 season, AS Roma set a historic record in Serie A by winning ten consecutive matches at the start of the season. This winning streak reflects not only the impeccable strategy and synergy of the team but also the determination and technical quality of the players, establishing Roma as a dominant force in Italian football.

2. The Highest Number of Career Assists

Xavi Hernández holds the impressive record for the highest number of career assists, with 356 assists. Throughout his career, mainly at FC Barcelona and the Spanish national team, Xavi demonstrated an exceptional vision of the game and an ability to deliver precise passes, significantly contributing to the success of his teams.

3. Real Madrid, 14 UEFA Champions League Wins

Real Madrid, with its 14 UEFA Champions League wins, embodies excellence and achievement in European football. This record illustrates a tradition of success and excellence, demonstrating the club's ability to remain at the top and compete with the best teams in Europe across decades.

4. Ryan Giggs, the Longest Career in the Premier League

Ryan Giggs, with his remarkable career spanning 23 seasons at Manchester United, established a record for longevity in the Premier League. His continuous presence from 1990 to 2014 not only symbolizes his talent and devotion to the club but also his ability to adapt and excel in one of the most demanding leagues in the world, marking the history of English football.

5. Ali Daei, International Goals Record

Ali Daei, the illustrious Iranian striker, set a historic milestone in international football by scoring 109 goals, a world record for international matches. His international career, spanning from 1993 to 2006, was marked by a goal-scoring efficiency rarely matched.

6 Brazil – Record of World Cup Appearances

Brazil, a country synonymous with football, holds a unique record in terms of presence at the FIFA World Cup, having participated in every edition of the tournament since its inception in 1930. This uninterrupted streak not only illustrates Brazil's passion and football tradition but also its consistent ability to produce world-class talent.

7 Manchester United, the Greatest Comeback in Premier League History

Manchester United, under the guidance of Sir Alex Ferguson, accomplished a memorable feat during the 1995-1996 Premier League season. By overcoming a 12-point deficit that separated them from Newcastle United, the Red Devils orchestrated the greatest comeback in the league's history. This season remains etched in the annals of English football as a testament to Manchester United's ability to defy the odds and triumph in crucial moments.

8 Javier Zanetti, Most Serie A Matches Played by a Non-Italian Player

Javier Zanetti, an icon of Inter Milan, has made history in Serie A by playing 615 matches, a record for a non-Italian player. His constant presence on the field for over two decades is a testament to his longevity, resilience, and commitment to the Milanese club. Zanetti, with his professionalism and leadership, has become an emblematic figure, embodying the values of loyalty and excellence in Italian football.

9 Francesco Totti, Most Goals for a Single Club in Serie A

Francesco Totti, the legend of AS Roma, holds the impressive record of scoring 250 goals in Serie A for a single club. This not only underscores his exceptional talent as a striker but also his unwavering commitment to Roma. Totti has personified the spirit and passion of Roman football, leaving an indelible mark on the history of the club and the Italian league.

10 Just Fontaine, Record for Most Goals in a Single World Cup

Just Fontaine, with his 13 goals during the 1958 World Cup, holds the record for the most goals scored in a single edition of the tournament. This extraordinary performance by the French striker remains unmatched, showcasing goal-scoring efficiency and positional sense that dazzled the football world. Fontaine has thus made history in the World Cup, setting a benchmark for future generations.

11. Peter Shilton, Most Matches Played in England

Peter Shilton, an iconic goalkeeper, set a monumental record with 1,005 professional matches played in England. His career, marked by consistency and excellence, has left an indelible imprint on the history of English football, demonstrating the importance of longevity and regular performance at the highest level.

12. Lionel Messi, Most Goals for a Single Club

Lionel Messi scored 672 goals for FC Barcelona, an astonishing record that reflects his offensive genius and dedication to the Catalan club. His consistent scoring ability has forged his legacy as one of the greatest talents football has ever seen.

13. Rogério Ceni, Most Goals Scored by a Goalkeeper

Rogério Ceni, legendary goalkeeper for São Paulo, revolutionized the goalkeeper role by scoring 131 goals, an unparalleled feat for a goalkeeper. His abilities as a free-kick and penalty taker not only contributed to his team's success but also redefined what is expected from a goalkeeper.

14. Miroslav Klose, All-Time Top Scorer of the World Cup

Miroslav Klose, with 16 goals, holds the record for the most goals scored in World Cup history. This achievement not only highlights his skill and opportunism in front of goal but also his ability to consistently perform on the biggest international stage. Klose has marked his era, becoming a model of longevity and efficiency, and leaving an indelible legacy in global football.

15. Arsenal, Undefeated Premier League Season (2003-2004)

Arsenal's 2003-2004 Premier League season is etched in history as one of the greatest feats in English football. Under Arsène Wenger's leadership, Arsenal finished the season without a single defeat, earning the nickname "The Invincibles." This exceptional performance is a testament to the quality of play, team cohesion, and Wenger's visionary strategy, establishing this Arsenal team as one of the most remarkable in the history of English football.

16. Cristiano Ronaldo, the First Player to Win Five UEFA Champions League Titles

Cristiano Ronaldo is an extraordinary footballer who has won the prestigious UEFA Champions League five times, first with Manchester United and then with Real Madrid. This exceptional record reflects his immense individual talent. Ronaldo is a decisive player who can change the course of matches and tournaments with his brilliance. His performances have marked recent football history, making him one of the greatest players of all time.

17. Xavi Hernandez, Player with the Most Wins in La Liga

Xavi Hernandez is a legend of FC Barcelona. A visionary midfielder, he played 505 La Liga matches, setting a record. As the mastermind of Barcelona's possession-based system, Xavi greatly contributed to Barça's era of dominance. Becoming a coach in 2021, he strives to impart his philosophy of play, focusing on technique, movement, and pressing. Despite a challenging start, Xavi has steered the club to the top of La Liga in 2023.

18. Claudio Taffarel, Goalkeeper with the Most Clean Sheets for Brazil

Claudio Taffarel, an iconic Brazilian goalkeeper, holds the record for the most matches without conceding a goal for the Brazilian national team. His reliability, reassuring presence between the posts, and key performances have played a crucial role in Brazil's success on the international stage, making him a benchmark in the history of goalkeepers.

19. Preston North End, First Undefeated Team in English Championship (1888-1889)

Preston North End made history by finishing the 1888-1889 season undefeated, achieving a perfect record in the very first English championship. During this historic season, the team played 22 matches, winning 18 and drawing 4. Scoring 74 goals and conceding only 15, their superiority was undeniable, laying the foundations of modern English football.

20. Gianluigi Buffon, Most Clean Sheets in Serie A

Gianluigi Buffon, a legendary goalkeeper, holds the record for the most clean sheets in Serie A. Out of 657 matches played in the Italian top flight, he managed not to concede a goal in 296 of them, a testament to his ability to lead his defense and make crucial saves. A pillar of Juventus and the Italian national team for over 20 years, Buffon has left an indelible mark on the history of Italian football with his longevity and exceptional performances.

21 Stephanie Roche, Finalist for the FIFA Puskás Award in 2014

In 2014, Stephanie Roche scored one of the most beautiful goals of the year with Peamount United, becoming the first woman finalist for the FIFA Puskás Award. Her brilliant volley from 20 meters dazzled the world and highlighted the exceptional talent present in women's football. Although she did not win the trophy, Roche paved the way for greater recognition of female players.

22 Gerd Müller, Record for Most Goals in a Bundesliga Season

The 1971-1972 season entered football legend as the ultimate consecration of Gerd Müller. Playing for Bayern Munich, the striker scored an astounding 40 goals in the Bundesliga, setting a record that long challenged the most prolific scorers. This stratospheric performance cemented his status as an extraordinary center-forward and a true scoring machine.

23 Spanish National Team, 35 Consecutive Matches Unbeaten

Between 2007 and 2009, La Roja achieved a resounding feat by remaining unbeaten for 35 consecutive matches, spanning more than two years without a loss. This staggering series of positive results illustrates the absolute domination of this golden generation of Spanish football at its peak. This record of longevity will remain etched in the annals of international football.

24 Mohamed Salah, Record for Most Goals in a Premier League Season (38 Matches)

In the 2017-2018 season, Mohamed Salah had a historic season with Liverpool, scoring 32 goals in the Premier League. The Egyptian shattered the record for the most goals in 38 matchdays in the English elite. His clear strikes, bewildering dribbles, and keen sense of goal dazzled fans. Named the best player and top scorer, Salah entered the legends of the Reds with his exceptional performances, which greatly contributed to Liverpool's brilliant season.

25 Most World Cups Won by a Coach

Vittorio Pozzo holds the exceptional record of being the only coach to have won two World Cups, leading Italy to triumph in 1934 and 1938. This unique achievement not only illustrates his tactical genius but also his indelible influence on football. These consecutive victories highlight Pozzo's expertise and strategy, marking his name in history as an architect of Italian football success.

26. The Longest Football Manager Game

A passionate Polish fan of Football Manager pushed the limits of the game by reaching the year 2434 in his save, amounting to 416 virtual seasons. This extraordinary performance showcases exceptional dedication and perseverance. A true marathon of video gaming, this feat required thousands of hours of intense gameplay. The fan thus broke all longevity records in this popular football management game, entering the legend of the Football Manager community in the process.

27. Eric Brook and Sergio Agüero, Joint Record Holders for Goals at Manchester City

Eric Brook and Sergio Agüero each scored 177 goals for Manchester City, setting an absolute record for the club. Brook achieved this total between 1928 and 1940, notably scoring 178 goals in 494 matches across all competitions. Agüero matched this number between 2011 and 2021, becoming the top scorer in Premier League history for the Cityzens with 184 goals. These two legendary strikers with impressive stats embody City's great offensive tradition.

28. Most Goals by a Team in a Single World Cup

The Hungarian national team set an impressive record during the 1954 World Cup in Switzerland by scoring 27 goals in total during the tournament. This offensive feat remains unmatched, highlighting the power and efficiency of the Hungarian attack during this historic competition.

29. Faryd Mondragón, Oldest Player to Participate in a World Cup

Faryd Mondragón made history at the 2014 World Cup in Brazil by becoming, at 43 years and 3 days old, the oldest player to play in a World Cup match. The Colombian goalkeeper defied time by playing in the final group match against Japan, 15 years after his first participation in 1998. A remarkable example of longevity for this veteran who guarded Colombia's goal for nearly 20 years. A record that is difficult to match.

30. Nicklas Bendtner (Arsenal, Premier League against Tottenham, December 22, 2007)

Bendtner set a remarkable record when he scored just 1.8 seconds after coming on as a substitute, in a highly anticipated derby between Arsenal and Tottenham. His instantaneous header from a corner not only secured the victory for Arsenal but also etched Bendtner's name in history as the scorer of one of the fastest goals by a substitute in Premier League history.

Technical Prowess in Women's Football

These exceptional athletes brilliantly demonstrate their skill, finesse, and game intelligence, inspiring a new generation of fans and players. Through breathtaking technical moves, bold dribbles, and precise finishes, women's football players embody excellence and innovation on the field.

1. Carli Lloyd - FIFA Women's World Cup Final 2015

Lloyd achieved a remarkable feat by scoring a hat-trick in the first 16 minutes of the final against Japan, including a sensational goal from midfield. This performance was crucial for the United States' victory and showcased her incredible talent and vision for the game.

2. Wendie Renard - Olympique Lyonnais

Renard, the iconic captain of OL, has been a key figure in her club's domination in Europe. Her defensive technique, aerial game, and ability to score from set pieces have been essential for the team's repeated success in the Women's Champions League.

3. Lieke Martens - UEFA Women's Euro 2017

Martens played a crucial role in the Netherlands' victorious campaign at Euro 2017, displaying refined technique, effective dribbling, and the ability to score important goals, significantly contributing to her national team's first major victory in a tournament.

4. Megan Rapinoe - FIFA Women's World Cup 2019

Rapinoe was one of the stars of the tournament, not only demonstrating her talent on the field with key goals and assists but also her ability to inspire her team. Her technical performances and leadership were decisive for the United States' success.

5. Sam Kerr - Chelsea Women

Kerr has showcased her exceptional technique and scoring instinct in the Women's Super League and on the European stage. Her off-the-ball movements, precise finishing, and ability to create scoring opportunities out of nothing have been vital for her club and highlight the high technical level of modern women's football.

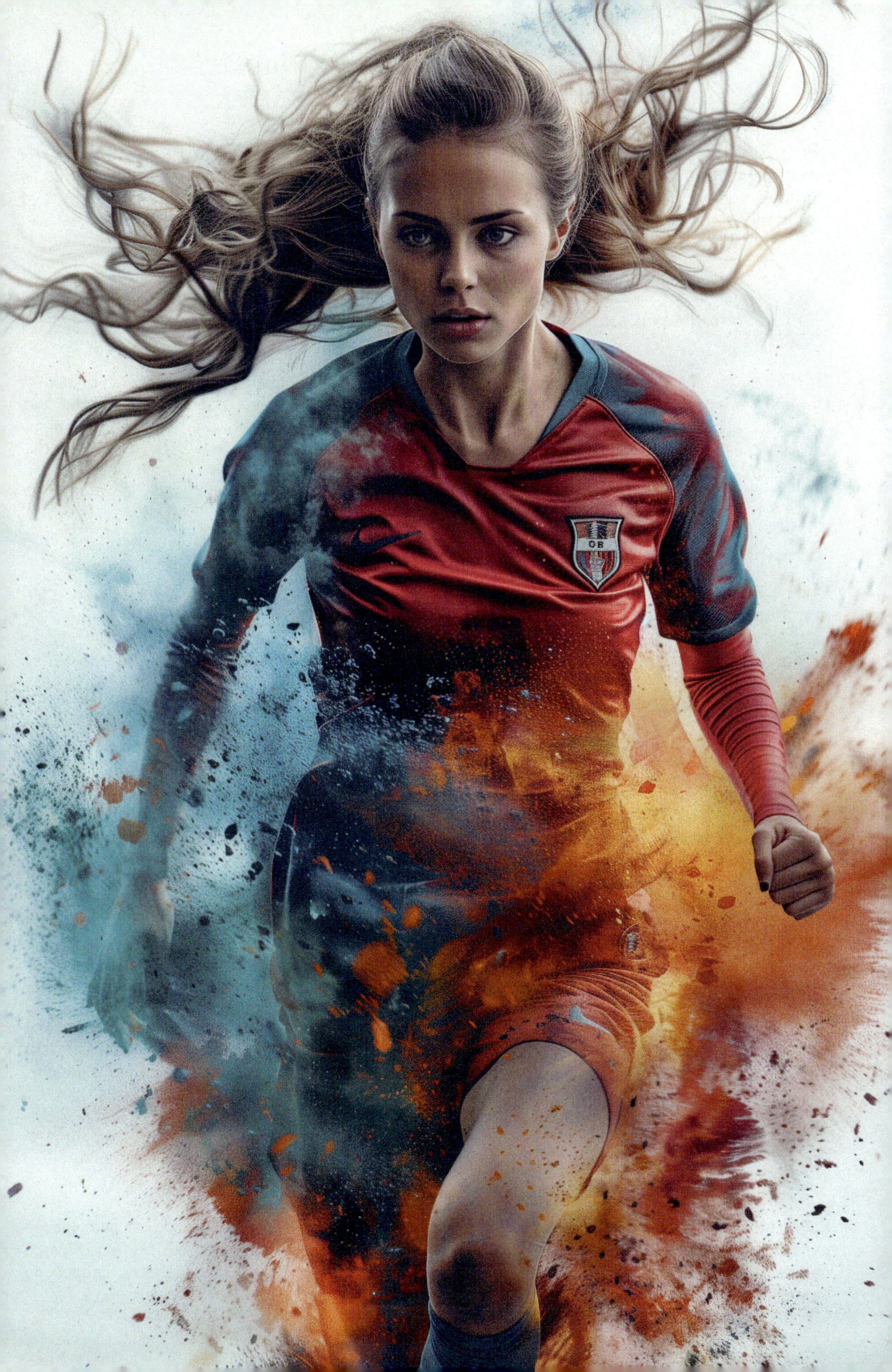

Historic Performances by Players

From breathtaking technical feats to time-defying records, each story celebrates the excellence and indelible impact of iconic players on the sport. Dive into the stories of figures such as Maradona, Messi, Pelé, and Zidane, and discover how their moments of glory continue to inspire the world of football.

1. Lionel Messi and His 91 Goals in 2012

In 2012, Lionel Messi achieved the unimaginable by scoring 91 goals in a calendar year, breaking the historic record of 85 goals set by Gerd Müller in 1972. Playing for FC Barcelona and the Argentine national team, Messi demonstrated remarkable versatility and efficiency, scoring in various competitions. This extraordinary feat cemented his place among football legends, showcasing his talent and unwavering determination.

2. Oleg Salenko – World Cup 1994

During the 1994 World Cup, Oleg Salenko entered history by scoring five goals in a single match, a feat achieved during the match between Russia and Cameroon. This unmatched performance not only set a world record but also highlighted an individual's capacity to profoundly influence the outcome of a match, making this moment one of the most memorable in World Cup history.

3. Pelé and His Three World Cups (1958, 1962, 1970)

Pelé, the Brazilian legend, remains unmatched with three World Cup victories (1958, 1962, 1970), a feat that defies imagination and has not been repeated since. These global triumphs not only proved his extraordinary talent but also left an indelible mark on football history, elevating Pelé to the status of a myth and a role model for future generations.

4. Zinedine Zidane and the 1998 World Cup, France

On July 12, 1998, Zinedine Zidane became a national hero in France, scoring two headers in the World Cup final against Brazil. This feat at the Stade de France not only gave France its first world title but also etched Zidane's name in the annals of football, symbolizing his elegance, vision, and impact on the game.

5. Roger Milla – Cameroon, World Cup 1990 and 1994

Roger Milla made history by becoming, at 38 in 1990 and at 42 in 1994, the oldest goal scorer in World Cup history. At the 1990 World Cup in Italy, he scored 4 goals, including a brace against Romania in the round of 16. His iconic goal celebrations and decisive impact on Cameroon's journey made him a symbol of longevity and excellence.

6 Kaká – AC Milan, UEFA Champions League 2006-2007

During the 2006-2007 UEFA Champions League season, Kaká, the Brazilian maestro of AC Milan, dazzled the football world with his breathtaking performances. As the cornerstone of the Milanese team, he led his club to the final victory against Liverpool in Athens. Scoring 10 goals in the competition, he finished as the tournament's top scorer, showcasing exceptional technical mastery and unparalleled game vision. His bewildering dribbles, ability to provide decisive assists, and memorable goals, particularly against Manchester United in the semi-finals, solidified his reputation and earned him the Ballon d'Or that same year.

7 George Weah, Ballon d'Or 1995

In 1995, George Weah made history by becoming the first African player to win the Ballon d'Or. His exceptional performances with AC Milan and Paris Saint-Germain transcended borders, making him a symbol of excellence in global football. His dynamic playing style and ability to score memorable goals made that year a cornerstone of his legendary career.

8 Lev Yashin, the Only Goalkeeper to Win the Ballon d'Or (1963)

Lev Yashin remains the only goalkeeper to have won the Ballon d'Or, an honor he received in 1963. Known for his spectacular saves, keen sense of positioning, and leadership, Yashin not only redefined his position but also set new standards of excellence for future generations, leaving an indelible mark on the history of Soviet and global football.

9 Michel Platini, Three Consecutive Ballons d'Or (1983-1985)

Michel Platini, with his elegance and vision for the game, dominated European football in the 1980s, winning the Ballon d'Or three times in a row (1983, 1984, 1985). This period illustrates his profound impact on the game, scoring decisive goals and orchestrating play from midfield with unmatched technical mastery, establishing a legacy that continues to inspire today.

10 Cristiano Ronaldo and His Five Ballon d'Or Awards

Cristiano Ronaldo, synonymous with excellence and perseverance, received his fifth Ballon d'Or in 2017, a reward that underscores his status among football icons. His victories in 2008, 2013, 2014, 2016, and 2017 reflect an exceptional career marked by successes with Manchester United, Real Madrid, and the Portuguese national team.

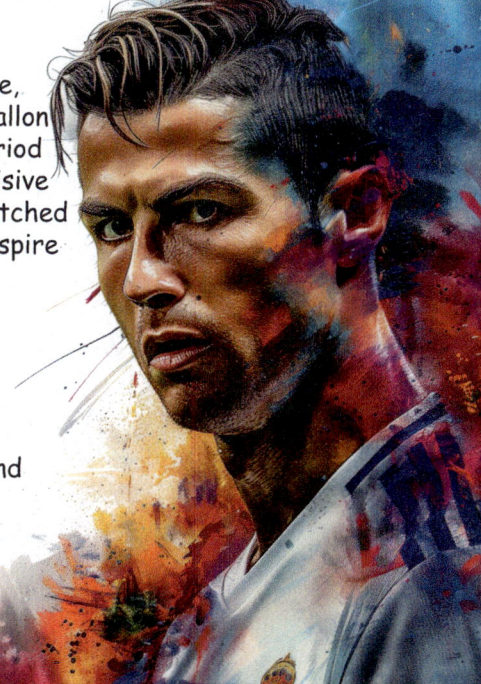

11 Paolo Maldini, a 25-Year Career at AC Milan

Paolo Maldini, the embodiment of elegance and leadership, dedicated his 25-year professional career exclusively to AC Milan. His presence on the field was synonymous with impregnable defense and timeless class. Winning countless titles, Maldini set standards for longevity and excellence, inspiring generations of defenders with his dedication and mastery of defensive play.

12 Ferenc Puskás, 84 Goals in 85 International Matches for Hungary

Ferenc Puskás is one of the greatest scorers in the history of football. With 84 goals in 85 appearances for Hungary, he boasts an exceptional average of 0.99 goals per match at the international level. A complete and opportunistic forward, Puskás notably scored 27 goals in 20 matches during the qualifiers and the final phase of the 1954 World Cup. His formidable efficiency makes him an absolute legend of Hungarian and global football.

13 Ronaldo Nazário (Inter Milan, Serie A 1997-1998)

In his first season at Inter Milan, Ronaldo delivered stunning performances, scoring 25 goals in Serie A and winning the Ballon d'Or. His dribbling, speed, and finishing captivated the football world, and his 1997-1998 season is often cited as one of the best individual performances in football history.

14 Franz Beckenbauer, Two-Time Ballon d'Or Winner and Libero Pioneer

Franz Beckenbauer, known as 'Der Kaiser', revolutionized football as a libero, a role he played with unprecedented elegance and tactical intelligence. A two-time Ballon d'Or winner and captain of the victorious 1974 German team, his successful transition to coaching, culminating in a World Cup title in 1990, reflects his exceptional influence and mastery of the game.

15 Marco van Basten, Sensational Goal in the Euro 1988 Final

Marco van Basten became a legend with an iconic goal in the Euro 1988 final against the Soviet Union. This goal, combining technique, audacity, and aesthetics, remains one of the most memorable in the history of the European Championships. Van Basten, with his ability to produce the extraordinary, left a lasting mark on his era and the collective memory of football.

Technological Advancements

These advancements not only enhance the precision of refereeing and optimize player performances; they also revolutionize the fan experience, making football fairer, more interactive, and more captivating than ever. Dive into a world where technology and football unite to push the limits of what's possible and shape the future of the world's most beloved sport.

1. VAR (Video Assistant Referee)

Introduced extensively during the FIFA World Cup 2018, VAR marked a turning point in football refereeing. By assisting referees in making more accurate judgments on crucial aspects of the game such as goals, penalties, direct red cards, and identity mistakes, VAR has significantly reduced human errors, thus promoting fairness and justice in the sport.

2. Hawk-Eye (Eagle Eye)

Inspired by its use in tennis, the Hawk-Eye system was adapted for football to precisely determine situations where the ball completely crosses the goal line. Officially deployed for the first time at the 2014 World Cup, it has put an end to controversies related to "ghost goals," bringing clarity and precision to refereeing decisions.

3. Performance Tracking Technology

The advent of wearable devices and GPS tracking systems has transformed performance analysis in football. These technologies enable real-time measurement of various indicators such as distance covered, speed, and acceleration of players, providing essential data for optimizing training and tactical strategies.

4. Smart Football Boots

The integration of electronic sensors in football shoes opens new prospects for game analysis. These "smart boots" collect data on speed, distance covered, and the accuracy of shots and passes, providing valuable information to enhance both individual and team performance.

5. Simulation and Virtual Reality

Virtual reality and 3D simulations offer players an innovative platform for training and tactical analysis. By enabling players to virtually relive match situations or experiment with different strategies, these technologies enhance mental preparation and understanding of the game, contributing to continuous performance improvement on the field.

Moments of Technical Brilliance

These feats of skill are not just mere actions; they are expressions of mastery and creativity that define the great artists of the beautiful game. From mesmerizing dribbles to strikes that defy the laws of physics, each exploit is a demonstration of players' abilities to push the boundaries of their art. Immerse yourself in moments where skill, ingenuity, and precision combine to deliver pure footballing genius.

1. Roberto Carlos against France (1997)

In 1997, Roberto Carlos defied the laws of physics with a free kick against France. With a powerful outside-left foot strike, the Brazilian full-back bent the ball in a stunning manner, curving around the wall and nestling into the opposite top corner of the French goal. The shot, from nearly 35 meters, swerved the ball almost supernaturally, fooling the helpless goalkeeper. A true stroke of genius, a perfect technical display that remains etched as one of the most beautiful free kicks in football history.

2. Gianfranco Zola (Chelsea vs. Norwich City, FA Cup 2001-2002)

During a 2002 FA Cup quarter-final, Gianfranco Zola delighted fans with a gem of Italian origin. Controlling the ball with his back to goal at the edge of the box, the Chelsea striker executed an impeccable bicycle kick to beat the opposing goalkeeper. A move full of class and audacity that demonstrates Zola's extraordinary technical quality at his peak. A brilliant inspiration that encapsulates the art of Italian football and the spirit of a player considered one of the best in Chelsea's history.

3. Zlatan Ibrahimović against England (2012)

In 2012 against England, Zlatan Ibrahimović scored one of the most improbable goals in history. Following a long clearance by the English goalkeeper, the Swede, with his back to goal, executed an incredible 30-meter bicycle kick, lobbing Hart with a move of wild technicality and audacity. A powerful aerial strike, almost unreal, that shook the English net with a moment of individual brilliance worthy of the greatest showmen in the game.

4. Ronaldo against Compostela (1996)

In 1996, Ronaldo delighted with a slalom worthy of the greatest. Against Compostela, the Brazilian striker picked up the ball in his own half and embarked on a series of stunning, decisive dribbles. Racing through defenders with feline agility at full speed, the "Phenomenon" combined power, speed, and technique to outplay the opposing defense. Arriving at the 18-yard box, he completed his masterpiece with a clear strike that left the goalkeeper stone-stoned.

5. Dennis Bergkamp, control and finish against Newcastle in 2002

In 2002, Bergkamp scored one of the most beautiful goals of his career against Newcastle. Receiving a through pass, the Dutch striker executed a world-class oriented control, resisting the defender's pressure to pivot and shake off his marker in a single elegant motion. After this technical display, Bergkamp concluded with a powerful right-foot shot that deceived the goalkeeper.

6 Gareth Bale against Barcelona (2014)

In the 2014 Copa del Rey final, Gareth Bale scored a goal of immense class against Barcelona. Starting from his left flank, the Welshman initiated a lightning-fast sprint that allowed him to completely outpace his direct defender with his phenomenal speed. Bale then perfectly controlled his run, avoiding going out of play or rushing his finish. Despite the immense pressure of a final, he concluded his solo effort with a powerful strike that deceived the goalkeeper, demonstrating great technical mastery.

7 Eric Cantona against Crystal Palace (1995)

In 1995, Eric Cantona's genius was once again on display with a goal of rare beauty. From a cross from the left, the Frenchman executed a superb chest control to cushion the ball. Instead of letting it drop, Cantona immediately followed with a majestic volley that blasted into the net. A move full of spontaneity and class, the ball barely grazed the grass. A true artist's goal that perfectly illustrated Cantona's unique technique and artistic sense of the game.

8 Ronaldinho against Villarreal (2006)

In 2006 against Villarreal, Ronaldinho produced a masterpiece that only he could conjure. Near the edge of the box, the Brazilian eluded the marking of two defenders with a sublime sequence of ground ball strikes. Facing the goal and noticing the momentarily distracted goalkeeper, the star then cheekily lobbed the keeper with a delicate chip that slowly rolled into the net. A move of incredible audacity, executed with remarkable technical finesse.

9 Jay-Jay Okocha against Arsenal (2003)

In a 2003 Premier League match, Jay-Jay Okocha dazzled with a dribbling display against Arsenal. Starting from his half of the field, the Nigerian rapidly executed body feints, changes of direction, and silky controls, baffling the opposing players who could not dispossess him. Okocha concluded this mesmerizing solo run with a strike that, while less spectacular, was effective. A masterpiece of its kind.

10 Neymar against Flamengo (2011)

In 2011, Neymar showcased his exceptional talent against Flamengo. Starting from the midfield line, the young Brazilian prodigy performed an incredible sequence of dazzling dribbles, bypassing a multitude of completely overwhelmed defenders. Weaving left and right and accelerating into the box, Neymar then perfectly finished his personal show with a sublime body feint to fool the goalkeeper before sliding the ball into the net. A brilliant action that summed up his incredible agility and overflowing creativity.

Technical and Tactical Innovations in Football

From the introduction of Dutch "Total Football" to the innovative approach of Catalan "Tiki-Taka," and the transformation of the goalkeeper's role with the "Sweeper-keeper," these innovations have enriched football's spectacle, offering new tactical and strategic dimensions.

1. Dutch "Total Football" in the 1970s

In the 1970s, the Netherlands national team and their coach Rinus Michels revolutionized football with the concept of "Total Football." Led by geniuses like Johan Cruyff, this system challenged fixed positions on the field. Players constantly exchanged roles and zones of play to create unpredictability and disorganize opposing defenses. This approach allowed fluid gameplay with incredible freedom of movement, far from traditional patterns.

2. Italian "Catenaccio"

In the 1960s, coach Helenio Herrera at Inter Milan popularized the revolutionary "Catenaccio," an ultra-rigid defensive system. The focus was on a low and compact block, meticulously organized behind the ball, with many players dedicated to defensive tasks. However, "Catenaccio" was not merely a defensive approach. On the rare occasions of losing the ball, attacks were launched at incredible speed to catch the opponent off guard.

3. FC Barcelona's "Tiki-Taka"

Under the guidance of Pep Guardiola, FC Barcelona revolutionized football with its unique style of play, "Tiki-Taka." Based on dominant ball possession, short and precise passing, and constant player movement, this philosophy of play led Barça to numerous titles between 2008 and 2012. The team, led by exceptional players like Lionel Messi, Xavi, and Andrés Iniesta, dazzled fans worldwide with its offensive and aesthetic football.

4. Jürgen Klopp's "Gegenpressing"

Jürgen Klopp, with his "Gegenpressing," transformed defensive strategy into a form of attack. At Dortmund and Liverpool, his teams applied immediate pressure after losing the ball, often regaining possession within 10 seconds of the turnover. This constant pressure confused opponents and led to significant victories, including the 2019 Champions League with Liverpool, where his team excelled in ball recovery and quick transitions.

5. Manuel Neuer's "Sweeper-keeper"

Manuel Neuer redefined the goalkeeper position with his "Sweeper-keeper" style. Venturing far from his goal, he intercepts long opposition balls and actively participates in building play, with over 1000 passes per season. A true initiator of attacks, Neuer provides additional defensive security for Bayern Munich and Germany. Combining technique, game vision, and positional sense, he has set new standards for modern goalkeepers.

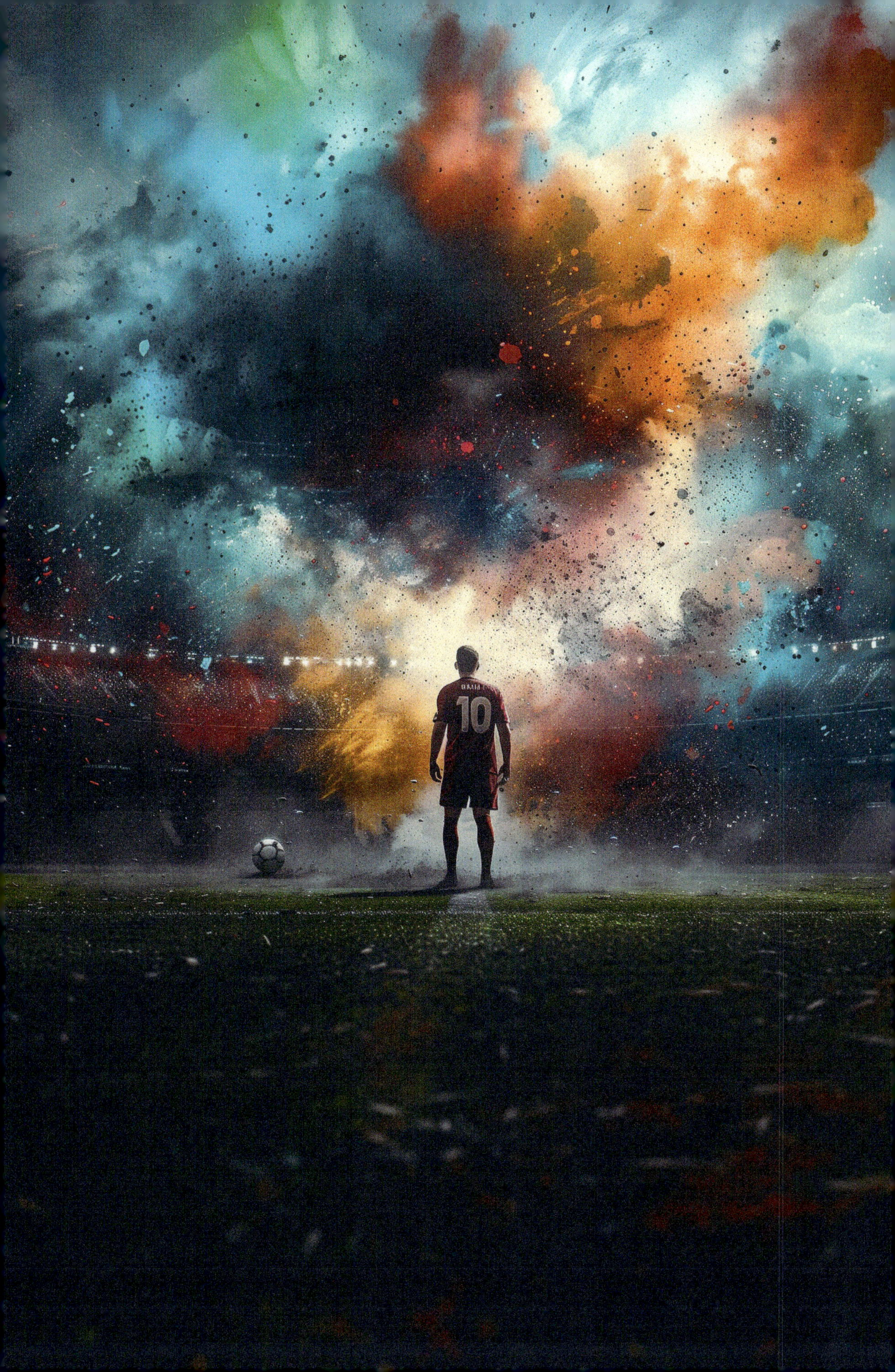
10

Career Pinnacles of Individual Players

Explore moments when players reached the pinnacle of their careers, marking performances that not only defined their legacy but also captivated fans worldwide. These moments of glory, the fruits of talent, dedication, and perseverance, illustrate what is possible when excellence meets opportunity on the grand stage of football.

1. Bobby Charlton (England, 1966 World Cup)

Charlton was a key figure in the England team that won the 1966 World Cup on home soil. His performances throughout the tournament, including crucial goals, were a peak in his international career, making him a legend of English football.

2. Ferenc Puskás (Real Madrid, European Champions Cup 1959-1960)

Ferenc Puskás was a central figure at Real Madrid, peaking during the 1959-1960 European Champions Cup final, where he scored four goals in the historic 7-3 victory against Eintracht Frankfurt. This performance in the final is one of the most memorable in football history, highlighting Puskás' ability to shine on the grandest stage. His contribution to Real Madrid during this period left an indelible mark, solidifying his status among football's most legendary strikers.

3. Alessandro Del Piero at Juventus, Iconic 1995-1996 Season

Alessandro Del Piero played a key role in Juventus' 1995-1996 Champions League triumph, contributing decisive goals and inspiring performances. His refined technique, game vision, and ability to deliver in critical moments were essential to Juventus' victorious campaign, marking the beginning of his long and illustrious career at the club and establishing Del Piero as an undisputed icon of the Old Lady.

4. Oliver Kahn and His Heroic Performance in the 2002 World Cup

Oliver Kahn was exceptional during the 2002 World Cup, earning the Best Goalkeeper award and the Golden Glove. His remarkable saves and leadership propelled Germany to the final. Despite a mistake on the first goal by Brazil in the decisive match, his influence and presence throughout the tournament enhanced his reputation, confirming him as one of the most distinguished goalkeepers of his era.

5. Luka Modric Winning the Ballon d'Or in 2018

Luka Modric, by winning the 2018 Ballon d'Or, broke the dominance of Messi and Ronaldo, rewarding a year in which he was instrumental in Real Madrid's Champions League success and led Croatia to a surprising World Cup final. His excellence in midfield management, game vision, and ability to influence matches under pressure were universally recognized.

6 Franz Beckenbauer (Bayern Munich and Germany)

Franz Beckenbauer, or "Der Kaiser," not only dominated but also redefined the libero role, leading Bayern Munich to three consecutive European Cup victories (1974-1976) and Germany to a World Cup victory in 1974. His style of play, characterized by elegance and tactical intelligence, transformed defensive standards, with Beckenbauer playing a crucial role in 104 national caps and significantly contributing to the successes of his club and country.

7 Ronaldo Nazário and His Formidable 2002 World Cup

Ronaldo "the Phenomenon" made history at the 2002 World Cup, scoring 8 goals and leading Brazil to their fifth world title. His performance in the final against Germany, where he scored two goals, became legendary, marking a triumphant return after battling serious injuries, and underscoring his place among the most talented strikers of all time.

8 Zinedine Zidane, His Legendary Goal in the 2002 Champions League Final

Zinedine Zidane's goal in the 2002 Champions League final for Real Madrid remains one of the greatest moments in the competition. This masterful left-footed volley not only sealed the victory against Bayer Leverkusen but also embodied Zidane's technical genius and creativity, cementing his reputation as one of the most skilled and inspiring players of his generation.

9 Johan Cruyff (Ajax and FC Barcelona)

Johan Cruyff was a stalwart for Ajax Amsterdam, winning three consecutive European Cups (1971-1973), and deeply influenced FC Barcelona as both a player and coach. His approach to football, marked by intelligence and innovation, has left a lasting legacy, affecting not only his teams but also the future evolution of the game, with a particularly notable influence on Barça's "Tiki-Taka" style.

10 Alfredo Di Stéfano (Real Madrid)

Alfredo Di Stéfano, an emblematic figure of Real Madrid, was crucial in the historic series of five consecutive European Cup wins (1956-1960). With his ability to play in almost any position on the field, Di Stéfano demonstrated extraordinary versatility and effectiveness, inscribing his name among football legends with an influence and impact that resonate well beyond his own era.

Did You Know?

1. The First International Football Match

The first international football match, played between Scotland and England in 1872, laid the foundation for international football, ushering in an era of competitions between nations. This goalless draw in Glasgow became a historic event, marking the start of a tradition that would lead to tournaments like the World Cup.

2. The Invention of Cards

Introduced in 1970 by Ken Aston to improve the communication of refereeing decisions, yellow and red cards revolutionized football officiating. This innovation not only clarified the rules of the game but also influenced discipline on the field, becoming a central element of modern refereeing.

3. The Longest Match

The current record, certified by Guinness World Records, is held by the teams SF Winterbach and TGIF-EC Wallhalben, who played for 168 consecutive hours (a full 7 days) in Winterbach, Germany, from May 29 to June 5, 2019. The final score was 1830 to 1797 in favor of TGIF-EC Wallhalben, with a total of 3627 goals scored. More than 30 referees took turns officiating this match.

4. Record for Most Goals in a Season

In 1959, at just 19 years old, Pelé achieved the incredible feat of scoring 127 goals in a single calendar year while playing for Santos. This absolute record has never been equaled and illustrates the early genius of the Brazilian prodigy. Capable of scoring against the world's greatest teams during his club's international tours, Pelé elevated the art of goal-scoring to a level never seen before, establishing himself as the greatest player of all time.

5. The Fastest Goal

Nawaf Al-Abed scored the fastest goal in the history of professional football just 2.4 seconds after kickoff. This remarkable achievement highlights the unpredictable nature of football and the speed at which a match can change.

6. The Most Expensive World Cup

The 2014 World Cup in Brazil, with estimated costs of $15 billion, remains the most expensive edition to date. This highlights the scale of investment required to host an event of such magnitude and the significant economic impact on the host country, as well as the global enthusiasm for this tournament.

7. The Largest Number of Spectators

The historic 1950 World Cup match between Brazil and Uruguay remains legendary not only for its surprising outcome but also for the incredible attendance of nearly 200,000 spectators. This record illustrates the unique passion and enthusiasm that football generates, capable of bringing together a vast crowd to share in the joy, anticipation, and sometimes, disappointment.

8. Football During War

The Christmas Truce of 1914, where German and British soldiers spontaneously played football, shows the universal ability of the sport to create bonds and provide a moment of respite and fraternity, even in the trenches of World War I. This impromptu match is a poignant testimony to shared humanity and the unifying power of football.

9. The Most Decorated Club

With 14 Champions Leagues, 35 Spanish league titles, and 5 Club World Cups, Real Madrid epitomizes football excellence. The club's continuous success, both on the national and international stages, demonstrates its ability to attract and nurture world-class talent, while inspiring fans around the globe.

10. The Oldest International Player

Isaak Hayik, by playing football at the age of 73, broke age-related barriers, demonstrating that passion for the game knows no limits. His feat underlines that football is a sport for all, regardless of age, celebrating the indomitable spirit of players who continue to pursue their love for the game.

11. The First Televised Match

The very first live broadcast of a football match dates back to September 16, 1937, in England. It was a friendly match between Arsenal and its reserve team, broadcast by the BBC. This event marked a turning point, transforming how fans experience and follow the sport. It laid the groundwork for football to become the most popular and most-watched sport in the world, with television playing a key role in its global expansion.

12. The Beginnings of Women's Football

The evolution of women's football, from its ban in 1921 to its rise as a global sporting phenomenon, illustrates the struggle for equality and recognition in sports. The progression of women's football is an inspiration, showing that determination and passion can overcome obstacles and change perceptions, leading to increased recognition and support for female athletes worldwide.

Undefeated Records

Explore the sagas of invincibility where players and teams have pushed the boundaries of perseverance, establishing records that showcase tenacity and continuous performance. These uninterrupted winning streaks are not just simple statistics; they tell stories of perseverance, tactics, and resilience.

1. Juventus and Its 49-Match Undefeated Streak in Serie A (2011-2012)

Under the tactical leadership of Antonio Conte, Juventus set an impressive record in Serie A by remaining unbeaten for 49 consecutive matches. This streak spanned from the end of the 2010-2011 season to the start of the 2012-2013 season, symbolizing the beginning of a period of supremacy in Italian football. With key figures like Gianluigi Buffon as the infallible goalkeeper, Andrea Pirlo orchestrating the play, and Arturo Vidal providing energy and versatility, Juventus demonstrated remarkable defensive and offensive consistency.

2. AC Milan and Its 58 Home Matches Undefeated in Serie A (1991-1996)

Under the guidance of Arrigo Sacchi and Fabio Capello, AC Milan established home dominance by remaining undefeated in 58 Serie A matches. This team, bolstered by legends like Franco Baresi, Paolo Maldini, and Marco van Basten, defined an era, combining exceptional defensive rigor with offensive efficiency. Their impact extended beyond Italy, influencing European football standards with their innovative playing style and tactical excellence.

3. FC Porto under José Mourinho (2002-2004)

José Mourinho transformed FC Porto into a dominant force, achieving an undefeated streak of 27 matches in the Primeira Liga during the 2002-2003 season and culminating with a Champions League victory in 2004. Mourinho instilled strict tactical discipline, with players like Deco and Ricardo Carvalho becoming key components of a team that was marked by its efficiency and cohesion, establishing itself as a European powerhouse.

4. Spain and Its 35-Match Undefeated Streak (2007-2009)

Spain set a new standard in international football with an undefeated streak of 35 matches, including their victory at Euro 2008. This team, led by Luis Aragonés and then Vicente del Bosque, perfected a style of play based on possession and movement, with talents such as Xavi Hernandez, Andrés Iniesta, and Iker Casillas, defining an era where tiki-taka became synonymous with tactical success and innovation.

5. Arsène Wenger and the "Invincibles" Arsenal (2003-2004)

Arsène Wenger's Arsenal achieved a historic feat in the Premier League by completing the 2003-2004 season without a single defeat. With 26 wins and 12 draws, the team demonstrated a perfect balance between blistering attack and solid defense, scoring 73 goals and conceding only 26. The performances of players like Thierry Henry, Patrick Vieira, and Dennis Bergkamp were central to this achievement, illustrating Wenger's innovative vision and his lasting impact on English football.

6. Italy and Its 37-Match Undefeated Streak (2018-2021)

The Italian national team, under Roberto Mancini, set a new European record with 37 matches undefeated, a streak that included their victory at Euro 2020. This period showcased talents like Leonardo Bonucci, Marco Verratti, and Gianluigi Donnarumma, illustrating a perfect blend of defensive solidity and offensive creativity. This historic run marked Italy's return to the pinnacle of European football, demonstrating tactical evolution and depth of talent.

7. Lionel Messi's Achievement of Scoring in 21 Consecutive La Liga Matches (2012-2013)

Lionel Messi set a spectacular record by scoring in 21 consecutive La Liga matches, netting a total of 33 goals and scoring against every team in the league that season. This feat underscores his ability to be consistently decisive, affirming his crucial role in FC Barcelona's success and reinforcing his status as one of the greatest players in history.

8. Bayern Munich and Its 23 Consecutive Wins Across All Competitions (2020)

Under the leadership of Hansi Flick, Bayern Munich achieved 23 consecutive victories, a streak that peaked with their triumph in the Champions League. With players like Robert Lewandowski and Thomas Müller in top form, Bayern displayed an offensive power and cohesion that dominated European football, highlighting a period of unprecedented success for the club.

9. Inter Milan and Its 17 Consecutive Serie A Wins (2006-2007)

Inter Milan achieved a feat in Serie A with 17 consecutive victories, a key moment of their victorious season under Roberto Mancini. This performance underscored their supremacy in Italy, with significant contributions from Zlatan Ibrahimović and Javier Zanetti, who played crucial roles in the demonstration of strength and strategy that characterized this period.

10. Real Madrid and Its 40-Match Undefeated Streak Across All Competitions (2016-2017)

Real Madrid, under Zinedine Zidane, set a Spanish record with 40 matches undefeated, including victories in La Liga and the Champions League. Stars such as Cristiano Ronaldo, Karim Benzema, and Sergio Ramos were central to this streak, displaying a balance between dynamic attack and solid defense, and playing a key role in securing prestigious double titles for the club during this season.

Amazing anecdotes

1. A Match Interrupted by a Parachutist

During a Serie A match in October 2019 between Sassuolo and Inter Milan, an unusual event captured everyone's attention: a parachutist landed on the pitch, temporarily interrupting the game. This incident occurred just as Romelu Lukaku, Inter Milan's striker, was preparing to take a penalty. Despite the unexpected interruption, Lukaku remained focused and successfully converted the penalty, contributing to his team's victory.

2. The First Match Under Artificial Lights

Bramall Lane in Sheffield hosted the first football match under artificial lighting in 1878, an innovation that paved the way for playing matches in the evening and marked a significant evolution in the accessibility of football.

3. The "Ghost Goal" of the 1966 World Cup

During the 1966 World Cup final between England and West Germany, a controversial moment occurred. Geoff Hurst's shot hit the crossbar and fell near the goal line. The Swiss referee, after consulting with the linesman, awarded the goal to England, although footage could never confirm whether the ball had fully crossed the line. This "ghost goal" has become one of the most debated in football history, especially since England ultimately won the match 4-2.

4. The World Cup and World War II

The cancellation of the World Cup during World War II in 1942 and 1946 highlights the profound impact of global events on football, pausing the sport's most prestigious tournament due to the extraordinary circumstances of the time.

5. The Club Founded by a King

The grant of the title "Real" to Real Madrid by King Alfonso XIII in 1920 illustrates the unique connection between football and royalty in Spain, giving the club a particular stature and recognition that have enriched its legacy.

6. A Dog Saves a Penalty

The unexpected intervention of a dog during a match in Argentina, where it deflected a penalty, is a charming example of football's unpredictability. This incident captivated media and fans' attention, demonstrating how unexpected moments can sometimes bring joy and humor to the sport.

7. The Record for the Shortest Match

In 2000, the match between Falkirk and Inverness Caledonian Thistle became the shortest football match in history, interrupted after just 21 seconds due to dense fog, highlighting how weather conditions can sometimes have an immediate and unexpected impact on games.

8. The Goal for Gender Equality

The crucial goal scored by Marianne Pettersen in 2001 had significance far beyond the pitch, directly influencing Norway's historic decision to provide equal pay for male and female national teams, setting an important milestone for equality in sports.

9. A Red Card After 2 Seconds

Lee Todd received a red card just 2 seconds after the start of a match for expressing his surprise with a swear word at the referee's whistle, establishing an unlikely record for the fastest expulsion in football.

10. Zidane and the Number 5

Zinedine Zidane chose the number 5 throughout his career in tribute to Enzo Francescoli, a player he admired in his youth, illustrating the influence of football heroes on subsequent generations of players.

11. The First Substitution in Football

Keith Peacock made history in 1965 as the first substitute used in professional English football, marking a significant change in the game's rules that added a new tactical dimension to football.

12. The Most Goals by a Goalkeeper

Rogério Ceni, with over 100 goals to his name, primarily from free kicks and penalties, revolutionized the role of goalkeepers, proving that they can contribute significantly to the score and not just to the defense of their goal.

Match Turnarounds

These captivating moments demonstrate the determination, courage, and ingenuity of teams that refuse to admit defeat, even in the face of the most discouraging deficits. From epic comebacks to dramatic finals, these turnarounds capture the essence of suspense and excitement in football, where every minute can change the destiny of a match and, sometimes, an entire season.

1. Manchester United vs. Bayern Munich, 1999 Champions League Final

In an epic turnaround in Barcelona, Manchester United scored two goals in stoppage time to defeat Bayern Munich. Teddy Sheringham and Ole Gunnar Solskjaer made history by scoring these crucial goals, allowing United to achieve a historic treble, a feat rarely seen in modern football.

2. Barcelona vs. Paris Saint-Germain, 2017 Champions League Round of 16

On a memorable evening at Camp Nou, FC Barcelona accomplished a nearly unthinkable feat in the Champions League by overturning a 4-0 deficit from the first leg against PSG. With a final score of 6-1, marked by Sergi Roberto's decisive goal in the 95th minute, Barça proved that the impossible can become reality in football.

3. Deportivo La Coruna vs. AC Milan, 2004 Champions League Quarterfinal

Deportivo La Coruna created one of the biggest surprises in Champions League history by overturning a 4-1 deficit from the first leg against AC Milan. Winning 4-0 in the second leg, thanks to key performances from Valerón, Luque, Fran, and an own goal by Kaladze, Deportivo demonstrated that determination and strategy could overturn the most unfavorable odds.

4. Tottenham Hotspur vs. Ajax Amsterdam, 2019 Champions League Semifinal

Tottenham, trailing 2-0 at halftime of the second leg and 3-0 on aggregate against Ajax, orchestrated a sensational second-half comeback. Lucas Moura, with a hat-trick, including the winning goal in the 96th minute, led Spurs to an unexpected final, illustrating the magic and uncertainty of European football.

5. Liverpool vs. AC Milan, 2005 Champions League Final

Liverpool's turnaround against AC Milan in 2005 remains one of the most legendary moments in football. Trailing 3-0 at halftime, the Reds mounted a fantastic comeback with three goals in six minutes from Gerrard, Smicer, and Alonso, before winning on penalties, highlighting one of the most memorable and dramatic finals in Champions League history.

6. Newcastle United vs. Arsenal, Premier League 2011

Newcastle United orchestrated one of the most spectacular comebacks in Premier League history by recovering from a 4-0 deficit to draw 4-4 against Arsenal. The second half saw the Magpies unleashed, capping their comeback with a memorable free kick from Cheick Tiote. This match remains etched as a demonstration of Newcastle's determination and fighting spirit.

7. Borussia Dortmund vs. Malaga, Champions League Quarterfinal 2013

In a scarcely believable scenario, Borussia Dortmund scored two goals in stoppage time to eliminate Malaga and advance to the Champions League semifinals. Late goals by Marco Reus and Felipe Santana transformed the Signal Iduna Park into an arena of celebration, showcasing Dortmund's perseverance and team spirit.

8. Crystal Palace vs. Liverpool, Premier League 2014

In a memorable match, Crystal Palace came back from 3-0 down to equalize 3-3 against Liverpool, a pivotal moment in the Reds' Premier League title race. The match, ending in an electric atmosphere at Selhurst Park, underscored the unpredictable and thrilling nature of English football.

9. AS Roma vs. FC Barcelona, Champions League Quarterfinal 2018

AS Roma achieved one of the most impressive comebacks in Champions League history by overcoming a 4-1 deficit from the first leg against Barcelona. Winning 3-0 at the Stadio Olimpico, Roma advanced to the semifinals, thanks to goals from Dzeko, De Rossi, and Manolas, embodying courage and determination.

10. Arsenal vs. Reading, League Cup 2012

Arsenal staged an epic comeback in the League Cup, overturning a 4-0 deficit to defeat Reading 7-5 after extra time. The emotionally charged match, full of twists and turns, saw the Gunners equalize in the dying moments of regular time before triumphing in extra time, illustrating Arsenal's persistence and offensive prowess.

Fair Play and Acts of Great Class

These moments underscore the beauty and honor that can emerge even in the fiercest competition, reminding us that football is much more than just a game. Through acts of generosity, honesty, and mutual respect, players, coaches, and teams demonstrate that fair play is a fundamental value that transcends scores and titles, forging a legacy that inspires fans and players around the world.

1. Paolo Di Canio against Everton, 2000

Paolo Di Canio, playing for West Ham, displayed a memorable act of fair play by refusing to take advantage of the injury of the Everton goalkeeper. Choosing to catch the ball instead of scoring, Di Canio epitomized sportsmanship, a gesture that earned him the FIFA Fair Play Award and the admiration of the global football community.

2. Miroslav Klose against Napoli, 2012

Miroslav Klose, in a match for Lazio against Napoli, demonstrated exceptional integrity by admitting he had used his hand to score. His confession led to the goal being disallowed, and his honesty was celebrated as an example of virtue and respect for the rules of the game, enhancing his status as a model sportsman.

3. Dani Alves' Sportsmanship, 2013

In response to an act of racism where a banana was thrown onto the pitch, Dani Alves responded with intelligence and defiance by eating the banana before continuing to play. Far from stooping to the level of the insult, his act was a powerful rebuttal to racism, turning a negative moment into a strong message against discrimination.

4. Aaron Hunt against Nuremberg, 2014

Aaron Hunt, forward for Werder Bremen, displayed great integrity by informing the referee that he had not been fouled in the penalty area, which led to the cancellation of a penalty in his favor. This action was hailed as an exemplary act of fair play, highlighting the importance of honesty in sports.

5. Casillas' Respect for Buffon, 2017

Iker Casillas showed great respect for Gianluigi Buffon during what appeared to be Buffon's last Champions League match. By being the first to applaud when Buffon was substituted, Casillas underscored the importance of mutual respect and camaraderie among players, even in the most intense competition, thus celebrating the spirit of sportsmanship and brotherhood that transcends rivalries.

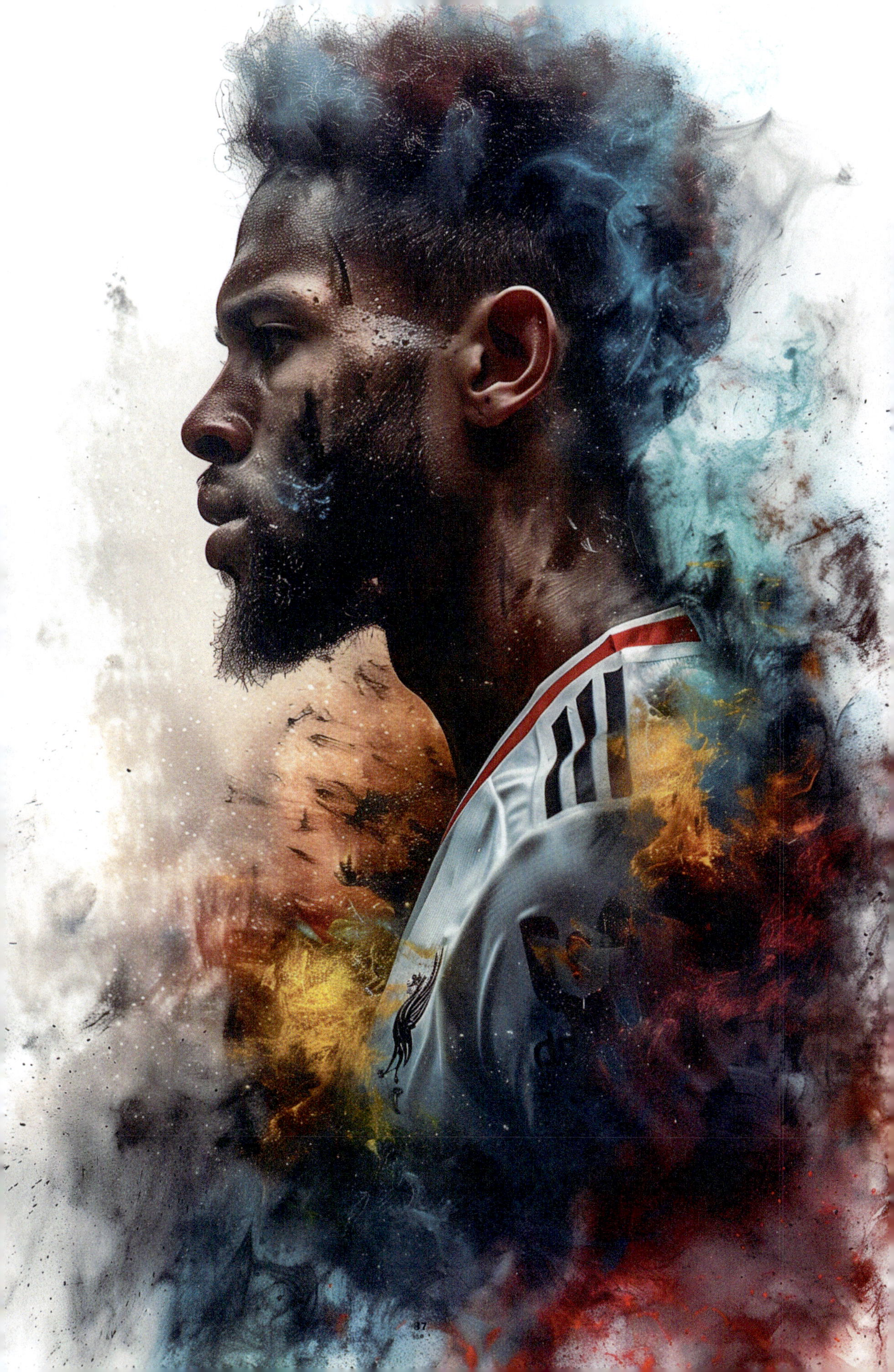

Legendary Performances in Finals

These finals, the ultimate stages where glory and disillusionment play out, have been showcases for talent, determination, and magical moments that have forever marked the history of football. Whether through a decisive goal, a series of spectacular saves, or flawless technical mastery, each player mentioned has etched their name into legend, turning these finals into memorable chapters in the grand book of football.

1. Diego Maradona, 1986 World Cup Final

Diego Maradona showcased why he is considered one of the greatest footballers of all time during the 1986 World Cup final. Though he didn't score, his influence on the game was decisive, especially with a masterful assist that helped Argentina secure a 3-2 victory over West Germany. His exceptional performance throughout the tournament, including his legendary goals in the quarterfinals and semifinals, was a key factor in Argentina's triumph.

2. Sergio Ramos, 2014 Champions League Final

Sergio Ramos delivered a legendary performance in the 2014 Champions League final against Atletico Madrid. His equalizing header in the 93rd minute not only saved Real Madrid from almost certain defeat but also pushed the match into overtime, where Real eventually triumphed 4-1. This crucial goal sparked the "Decima," Real Madrid's tenth victory in the competition, and solidified Ramos's reputation as a decisive player in critical moments.

3. Steven Gerrard, 2006 FA Cup Final

Steven Gerrard gave an unforgettable performance in the 2006 FA Cup final, rescuing Liverpool from near-certain defeat against West Ham with a sensational long-range goal at the end of the match. His energy, commitment, and ability to excel in critical moments were crucial for Liverpool to eventually win the trophy on penalties.

4. Lionel Messi, 2009 Champions League Final

Lionel Messi played a pivotal role in FC Barcelona's victory in the 2009 Champions League final by scoring with his head against Manchester United. This goal not only showcased his versatility and exceptional talent but also contributed to Barcelona's historic treble that season, affirming Messi's status as one of the most influential players in the world.

5. Carli Lloyd, 2015 Women's World Cup Final - USA vs Japan

Carli Lloyd delivered a legendary performance in the 2015 Women's World Cup final, scoring a hat-trick in just 16 minutes against Japan, a record in the history of World Cup finals, for both men and women. Her most memorable goal was her third, a long-range shot from midfield, demonstrating not only her incredible technique but also her confidence and vision of the game. This performance greatly contributed to the USA's 5-2 victory, making a mark in the history of women's football.

6. Frank Lampard, 2009 FA Cup Final - Chelsea vs Everton

Frank Lampard was instrumental in Chelsea's victory in the 2009 FA Cup final against Everton. Although the Blues were trailing from the first minute, Lampard turned the game around with an exceptional goal in the 72nd minute, demonstrating his ability to take responsibility in crucial moments. His powerful shot from outside the box sealed the 2-1 win for Chelsea, giving the team their fifth FA Cup title. This performance highlighted Lampard's role as a key player.

7. Mario Götze, 2014 World Cup Final

Mario Götze made history by scoring the decisive goal in the 2014 World Cup final against Argentina, crowning Germany as world champions. His technique in controlling and finishing a cross from Schürrle in extra time was a feat of precision and composure, making him a national hero and a symbol of Germany's victory in Rio.

8. Eusébio, 1962 European Cup Final

Eusébio played a key role in Benfica's triumph in the 1962 European Cup final against Real Madrid. Scoring two essential goals, he allowed his team to turn the game around and win 5-3. This performance solidified Benfica's status on the European stage and confirmed Eusébio's reputation as one of football's great legends.

9. Andrés Iniesta, 2010 World Cup Final

Andrés Iniesta was Spain's hero by scoring the winning goal in the 2010 World Cup final against the Netherlands. His goal in extra time not only gave Spain their first world title, but also illustrated his essential role and exceptional contribution within the team, etching his name in football history.

10. Diego Milito, 2010 Champions League Final vs Bayern Munich

Diego Milito was Inter Milan's hero in the 2010 Champions League final, scoring both goals in the 2-0 victory over Bayern Munich. His performance was crucial in securing Inter's historic treble that season.

Exceptional Tournament Performances

These exploits illustrate moments where talent, determination, and passion combine to create unforgettable memories, whether through legendary goals, decisive saves, or inspiring acts of leadership. Through these stories, we celebrate the players who have shone in the greatest competitions, demonstrating a level of excellence that defines careers and forges legends in the world of football.

1. Eusébio at the 1966 World Cup

Eusébio, the Portuguese legend, shone brightly during the 1966 World Cup, finishing the tournament as the top scorer with 9 goals. His most remarkable feat took place during the match against North Korea, where, after a disastrous start with a three-goal deficit, Eusébio took matters into his own hands, scoring four times to turn the score in Portugal's favor, winning 5-3.

2. Michel Platini at Euro 1984

The French playmaker had an exceptional tournament, scoring 9 goals in just 5 matches. A record that has never been equaled since in a European Championship. His influence was decisive, particularly during key moments such as the semi-final against Portugal, where his goal in extra time sent France to the final. Platini was not only a goalscorer but also a creator, orchestrating the game with a vision and precision that left an indelible mark on the history of European football.

3. Paolo Rossi at the 1982 World Cup

Paolo Rossi, after a discreet start to the tournament, transformed into a true goal-scoring machine starting from the decisive match against Brazil, where his hat-trick eliminated the favorites and etched his name in legend. With 6 goals, he finished as the tournament's top scorer, playing a crucial role in Italy's victorious run and proving that great players reveal themselves in big occasions.

4. James Rodríguez at the 2014 World Cup

James Rodríguez, with 6 goals, was the revelation of the 2014 World Cup, captivating spectators with his talent. His goal against Uruguay, a masterful volley after a chest control, was voted the tournament's best goal. Beyond his goals, he demonstrated a technique and vision of the game that propelled him among the world's best players.

5. Fabio Cannavaro at the 2006 World Cup

Fabio Cannavaro was the pillar of the Italian defense during the 2006 World Cup, where his play was synonymous with solidity, tactical intelligence, and leadership. His exceptional performance was crucial in Italy's path to victory, and he was rewarded with the Ballon d'Or the same year, a rare honor for a defender, highlighting his influence and defensive mastery throughout the tournament.

6. Roberto Baggio - Italy, 1994 World Cup

Roberto Baggio, with his transcendent talent, carried Italy to the 1994 World Cup final, scoring five goals along the way. Despite the tragic ending where his missed penalty sealed Italy's fate in the final against Brazil, Baggio remains celebrated for his footballing artistry, vision, and ability to produce moments of magic, illustrated by his key goals and undeniable influence on his team's journey.

7. Abby Wambach - 2011 FIFA Women's World Cup

Abby Wambach scored 4 goals and delivered 1 assist in 6 matches. Her most memorable goal came in the quarter-final against Brazil. With the Americans trailing 2-1 in stoppage time, Wambach equalized with a superb diving header from a Megan Rapinoe cross in the 122nd minute. This goal allowed the United States to force extra time and then win on penalties.

8. Geoff Hurst at the 1966 World Cup

Geoff Hurst entered the history books by becoming the first and only player to date to score a hat-trick in a World Cup final, leading England to victory in 1966. His second goal, shrouded in controversy over its validity, remains a subject of intense debate. However, Hurst's overall performance was a key factor in England's historic triumph on home soil.

9. Mario Kempes at the 1978 World Cup

Mario Kempes, with 6 goals, was the main architect of Argentina's success at the 1978 World Cup, particularly with his two decisive goals in the final against the Netherlands. His ability to stand out in crucial moments not only cemented his reputation as an exceptional goalscorer but also played a central role in securing Argentina's first world title.

10. Salvatore Schillaci - 1990 World Cup

Propelled from obscurity to international stardom, Salvatore Schillaci captivated Italy and the entire world during the 1990 World Cup. A substitute at the start of the tournament, he quickly proved indispensable, finishing as the top scorer with six goals and winning the tournament's Golden Ball award.

Decisive Victories Under Pressure

These captivating moments showcase teams and players who, faced with adversity, reveal extraordinary courage and determination to turn the tide of the game. Whether it's tense finals, improbable comebacks, or hard-fought qualifications, each story is a celebration of the competitive spirit that defines the great legends of football.

1. Liverpool vs. Olympiacos, 2004-2005 Champions League

In a crucial Champions League match, Liverpool, trailing 1-0 at half-time against Olympiacos, needed to win by a two-goal margin to qualify. The second half saw the Reds stage a remarkable turnaround, capped off by a spectacular goal from Steven Gerrard in the 86th minute, sealing a 3-1 victory. This decisive moment not only secured Liverpool's qualification but also marked the beginning of their heroic path to triumph in Istanbul.

2. Chelsea vs. Bayern Munich, 2012 Champions League Final

In a match where they were considered the underdogs, Chelsea managed to hold Bayern Munich to a draw in their own stadium, forcing the game into a penalty shootout after a crucial equalizer from Didier Drogba. Drogba then turned hero by scoring the decisive penalty, delivering Chelsea their first Champions League title in the most dramatic of scenarios.

3. Italy vs. France, 2006 World Cup Final

The 2006 World Cup final between Italy and France was settled by a penalty shootout after a 1-1 draw. In an atmosphere charged with emotion and tension, Italy displayed ruthless precision in their penalty execution, clinching the world title in a duel that will remain etched in memory.

4. Uruguay vs. Ghana, 2010 World Cup Quarter-Final

This quarter-final was marked by one of the most controversial moments in World Cup history when Luis Suárez saved a certain Ghanaian goal with his hand on the goal line. Uruguay then went on to win the penalty shootout, continuing their journey in the tournament under circumstances that sparked intense debate in the football world.

5. Manchester City vs. Queens Park Rangers, 2012 Premier League

Sergio Agüero's goal for Manchester City against QPR in the dying moments of the match has gone down in Premier League history. The goal not only secured City's victory but also sealed their first Premier League title in 44 years, coming in a context where every second counted and tension was at its peak.

6. Ghana - 2009 FIFA U-20 World Cup

In 2009, Ghana became the first African country to win a FIFA World Cup. In the final of the U-20 World Cup in Egypt, the Black Satellites defeated the heavily favored Brazil on penalties after a 0-0 draw. Despite the early dismissal of Daniel Addo, the Ghanaians resisted heroically before prevailing in the penalty shootout. Dominic Adiyiah finished as the top scorer with 8 goals. A historic triumph for African football.

7. Manchester United - 1998/1999 Champions League

The 1999 Champions League final saw Manchester United achieve one of the most spectacular comebacks in football history. Trailing Bayern Munich until stoppage time, the Red Devils scored two goals in quick succession, turning the score around to win the title. This incredible triumph illustrates the team's perseverance and unwavering belief in victory until the final whistle.

8. Australia vs. Uruguay, 2006 World Cup Qualifying Playoff

Australia overcame the pressure and immense stakes of World Cup qualification in the playoff against Uruguay. In Sydney, after a tense match and a 1-1 aggregate score, the footballoos triumphed on penalties, with goalkeeper Mark Schwarzer playing a crucial role. This match marked a turning point for Australian football, ending decades of waiting for a return to the world stage.

9. Netherlands vs. Mexico, 2014 World Cup Round of 16

In a stunning turnaround, the Netherlands, trailing Mexico until the final minutes, found the resources to reverse the trend. With goals from Wesley Sneijder and a penalty from Klaas-Jan Huntelaar in added time, the Dutch demonstrated incredible resilience and an ability to fight until the last second, captivating fans worldwide with their fighting spirit.

10. Zambia - 2012 Africa Cup of Nations

In 2012, Zambia achieved a resounding feat by winning the Africa Cup of Nations for the first time in their history. In the final against heavy favorites Ivory Coast, the Chipolopolo forced a penalty shootout after a goalless draw. Despite the pressure, the Zambians scored all 8 of their penalties, while Gervinho missed his for the Ivorians. A historic and emotional triumph, dedicated to the victims of the 1993 air tragedy.

Young Talent Prowess

These prodigies of the beautiful game have made their mark with exceptional performances from their very first steps in major competitions. From the audacity of a precocious striker to the serenity of a young goalkeeper, these talents demonstrate that the future of football is as promising as it is exciting.

1. Kylian Mbappé at the 2018 World Cup

Kylian Mbappé, at just 19 years old, illuminated the 2018 World Cup with his lightning speed and exceptional talent, scoring 4 goals and providing decisive play that was crucial to the success of the French team. His goal in the final against Croatia made him the second youngest player after Pelé to score in a World Cup final, a feat in the history of the tournament. His performance not only contributed to France's 4-2 victory but also established Mbappé as one of the leading talents in world football.

2. Lionel Messi with FC Barcelona in 2005

At the age of 17, Lionel Messi began captivating the football world with FC Barcelona, displaying abilities that already distinguished him as a future best player in the world. At that time, he not only scored crucial goals but also demonstrated an ability to play in a team of stars, making his way into the first team with impressive ease and confidence. His debut signaled the emergence of a player who would redefine modern football with his dribbling, vision, and unique ability to score and create chances.

3. Wayne Rooney with Everton and Manchester United

Wayne Rooney shone on the Premier League stage at 16, becoming the youngest goalscorer in league history at the time with a sensational goal against Arsenal. His transfer to Manchester United saw the young talent become a legend, where he accumulated a myriad of titles, including 5 Premier League titles and a Champions League, while becoming the club's second all-time leading scorer with 253 goals in 559 appearances, proving his status as a prodigy of English football.

4. Pelé at the 1958 World Cup

At just 17 years old, Pelé became the revelation of the 1958 World Cup, scoring six goals that were essential to Brazil's first triumph. His natural talent, vision, and finishing were decisive, especially in the final where his two goals cemented the 5-2 victory over Sweden. This tournament not only launched Pelé on the path to international glory but also set a new standard for what a young player can achieve on the world stage.

5. Cesc Fàbregas at Arsenal

Cesc Fàbregas, joining Arsenal's first team at 16, quickly became a midfield maestro, significantly contributing to the team's performances with his intelligence, vision, and passing accuracy. His rapid rise was punctuated by memorable moments, including becoming Arsenal's youngest goalscorer in the Champions League. With over 200 appearances for Arsenal before the age of 24, Fàbregas solidified his reputation as one of the most talented midfielders of his generation.

6 Erling Haaland au RB Salzburg et Borussia Dortmund

Erling Haaland a captivé le monde du football dès son apparition sur la scène internationale avec le RB Salzburg, notamment en Ligue des Champions où il a marqué 8 buts en 6 matchs de groupe, une performance remarquable pour un joueur de 19 ans. En moins d'une demi-saison, il a accumulé 16 buts en 18 matchs toutes compétitions confondues avec Dortmund, affirmant sa réputation de phénomène du football mondial.

7 Jude Bellingham à Borussia Dortmund

Arrivé à Dortmund à 17 ans, Jude Bellingham a immédiatement impressionné par son talent et sa maturité sur le terrain. Devenant rapidement un pilier du milieu de terrain, Bellingham a contribué significativement à la dynamique de l'équipe, participant à de nombreuses rencontres en Bundesliga et en Ligue des Champions. Sa capacité à s'adapter à un haut niveau de compétition, à exécuter des tâches défensives et offensives, et à montrer une compréhension tactique avancée, a souligné son potentiel immense et son statut de l'un des jeunes talents les plus prometteurs d'Europe.

8 Ansu Fati au FC Barcelone

Ansu Fati a fait irruption dans l'équipe première du FC Barcelone à seulement 16 ans, devenant le plus jeune buteur de l'histoire du club en Liga. Ses débuts ont été marqués par des performances impressionnantes, où sa vitesse, sa technique et sa finition ont été mises en avant. En battant des records de précocité et en démontrant une aptitude à s'adapter et à exceller au plus haut niveau, Fati a non seulement inspiré les fans du Barça mais a aussi été perçu comme une étoile montante du football mondial.

9 Gianluigi Donnarumma à l'AC Milan

Gianluigi Donnarumma est devenu le gardien titulaire de l'AC Milan à l'âge de 16 ans, une ascension spectaculaire pour un poste généralement dévolu à des joueurs plus expérimentés. Sa taille, ses réflexes, et sa capacité à effectuer des arrêts décisifs l'ont rapidement établi comme l'un des meilleurs jeunes gardiens au monde. Sa contribution à Milan et son impact immédiat ont suscité des comparaisons avec de grands noms du football italien, prouvant que Donnarumma n'était pas seulement un talent prometteur mais un joueur clé.

10 Martin Ødegaard au Real Madrid et à la Real Sociedad

Martin Ødegaard a rejoint le Real Madrid à 16 ans avec un poids d'attentes énormes. Ødegaard a démontré sa capacité à influencer le jeu au plus haut niveau. Avec des performances clés en Liga, illustrées par ses contributions en buts et en passes décisives, il a validé les espoirs placés en lui, montrant une maturité et une vision du jeu qui le distinguent parmi les jeunes talents du football européen.

Singular Moments of Brilliance

These individual feats, ranging from sensational goals to breathtaking solo efforts, celebrate players' ability to transcend expectations and leave their mark on the game through their creativity, technique, and audacity. These narratives explore how a moment of genius can immortalize a player, etching their name in the annals of football history.

1. Ronaldinho, FC Barcelona vs Chelsea, Champions League 2005

Ronaldinho captivated the football world with his phenomenal goal against Chelsea, where his technical genius was fully displayed. With a feint that left the defenders petrified and a toe-poke strike as precise as it was unexpected, he scored a goal that remains a pure manifestation of creativity and innovation, underlining his status as an artist on the field.

2. George Weah, AC Milan vs Hellas Verona, Serie A 1996

George Weah achieved a remarkable solo feat against Hellas Verona, where he recovered the ball near his own penalty area before traversing the entire pitch, eliminating several opponents with his speed and power. His perfect finish capped off an epic run, making this goal one of the greatest demonstrations of individual strength and talent in football history.

3. Wayne Rooney, Manchester United vs Manchester City, 2011 Premier League

Wayne Rooney's acrobatic overhead kick in the Manchester derby remains etched as a moment of pure inspiration. In a tight match, Rooney found a way to transcend, scoring a goal that not only gave Manchester United the victory but was also celebrated worldwide for its audacity and beauty, embodying the spirit of spectacular football.

4. Diego Maradona, Argentina vs England, 1986 World Cup

Diego Maradona immortalized his genius at the 1986 World Cup with a legendary goal against England, often cited as the "Goal of the Century". Maradona captivated the world by dribbling past half of the English team before scoring, a moment that symbolizes not only his extraordinary talent but also served as a turning point in Argentina's victorious journey in the tournament.

5. Saeed Al-Owairan, Saudi Arabia vs Belgium, 1994 World Cup

Al-Owairan achieved a remarkable feat by dribbling past several Belgian players from his own half before scoring during the group stage. This goal is often compared to Maradona's in 1986, due to its spectacular solo nature.

6 Michael Owen, England vs Argentina, 1998 World Cup

In an intense match against Argentina, 18-year-old Michael Owen left an indelible mark with an extraordinary goal. His slalom through the Argentine defense, capped by a powerful strike, not only showcased his incredible talent and speed but also signaled his rise as one of the future stars of world football.

7 Carlos Alberto, Brazil vs Italy, 1970 World Cup Final

Carlos Alberto's goal in the 1970 World Cup final against Italy remains one of the most beautiful in World Cup final history. The perfect conclusion to a collective play sequence by Brazil, his powerful strike after a series of passes sealed a 4-1 victory, celebrating football as an art form.

8 Henrik Larsson, Celtic vs Porto, 2003 UEFA Cup Final

Despite his team's loss, Henrik Larsson shone in the 2003 UEFA Cup final against Porto. His two headed goals, marked by a keen sense of positioning, highlighted his exceptional talent and impact at Celtic, bolstering his reputation as a key player and club legend.

9 Eden Hazard (Chelsea, Premier League vs Arsenal, 2017)

Eden Hazard dazzled spectators with a memorable goal against Arsenal in 2017. Starting from his own half, he weaved through Arsenal's defense with a combination of speed, technique, and power, before finishing with a remarkable goal. This individual action not only illustrated his exceptional talent but also marked a highlight of his Premier League career.

10 Thierry Henry - Goal against Manchester United, 2000

In the Premier League in 2000, Thierry Henry scored one of the most spectacular goals of his career against Manchester United. Receiving a long pass, the French striker controlled the ball with his chest, back to goal, turned around, and unleashed a powerful volley without even looking at the goal. The curling shot ended in the far corner, leaving goalkeeper Fabien Barthez powerless. A gesture of incredible spontaneity and perfect technique, demonstrating all of Henry's genius.

11. Cristiano Ronaldo, Real Madrid vs Porto, Champions League 2009

Cristiano Ronaldo left his mark in a Champions League match against Porto in 2009 with a stunning goal from nearly 40 meters out. His powerful shot cleaved through the air to find the top corner, leaving Porto's goalkeeper powerless and the spectators astonished. This goal, one of the most remarkable of his career, showcases his ability to make a difference at crucial moments and to score from virtually anywhere on the field.

12. Ryan Giggs, Manchester United vs Arsenal, FA Cup 1999

Ryan Giggs produced a moment of pure magic in the FA Cup semi-final against Arsenal. After intercepting a pass in his own half, he slalomed through several defenders before delivering a powerful strike. This decisive goal not only advanced Manchester United to the final but was also a key moment in their historic treble, highlighting Giggs' individual brilliance in critical moments.

13. Gareth Bale, Champions League Final 2018

Gareth Bale made Champions League history with an extraordinary goal in the final against Liverpool. Coming on as a substitute, he executed a spectacular bicycle kick, catapulting the ball into the net and leaving the stadium in awe. This legendary goal played a crucial role in Real Madrid's 3-1 victory, illustrating Bale's ability to excel in major events.

14. Lionel Messi, Barcelona vs Getafe, Copa del Rey 2007

Lionel Messi dazzled the football world with an unforgettable goal against Getafe in 2007, drawing comparisons to Diego Maradona's famous 1986 goal. Starting from his own half, Messi dribbled past several opponents with disconcerting ease before finishing his feat with a magnificent goal, highlighting his exceptional talent and ability to change the course of a match.

15. Robin van Persie - Diving Header against Spain, World Cup 2014

In the opening match of the 2014 World Cup, the Netherlands dealt a historic defeat to reigning champion Spain (5-1). Trailing 1-0, the Dutch equalized just before halftime with a sublime goal from Robin van Persie. On a long pass, the striker dived to catapult the ball with his head over a stunned Iker Casillas. This legendary goal, which became a symbol of the match, was the prelude to Spain's collapse and made a lasting impression on the tournament.

Tactical Masterworks of Coaches

This exploration shines a light on visionary coaches whose innovative approaches and bold decisions have not only shaped the destiny of their teams but have also influenced the evolution of the game itself. From implementing revolutionary game systems to strategic adaptations against formidable opponents, these tacticians have demonstrated that success in football relies as much on intelligence and preparation as on talent and technique.

1. Arrigo Sacchi at AC Milan

Arrigo Sacchi revolutionized football with his innovative approach at AC Milan, instituting a game based on high pressing, rigorous zone marking, and an offensive play centered around possession and movement. Milan dominated Italian and European football, winning multiple Serie A titles and consecutive Champions League titles in 1989 and 1990. His impact goes beyond trophies, influencing generations of coaches and changing the way the game is perceived and played.

2. Johan Cruyff at FC Barcelona

Johan Cruyff transformed FC Barcelona by instilling a game philosophy focused on possession, movement, and attack, principles that laid the groundwork for the future tiki-taka. His "Dream Team" of the 1990s won numerous titles, including the club's first European Cup in 1992. Cruyff's influence on Barça is indelible, marking an era of success and inspiring a tradition of attractive and dominant football.

3. Pep Guardiola at FC Barcelona

As a coach, Pep Guardiola elevated Barcelona's game to unprecedented levels, refining Cruyff's vision to create a team that dominated the world with its style of possession and pressing. Under his leadership, Barcelona won multiple titles, including several Champions Leagues. Guardiola not only continued Cruyff's legacy but also enriched it, influencing global football with his innovative ideas.

4. José Mourinho at Inter Milan

José Mourinho left an indelible mark at Inter Milan by leading the club to a historic treble in 2010. With an adaptive tactical style and a keen attention to detail, Mourinho transformed Inter into a winning machine, capable of triumphing under various circumstances and dominating Europe, marking one of the most glorious periods in the club's history.

5. Carlo Ancelotti at AC Milan and Real Madrid

Carlo Ancelotti is a renowned coach who has managed major European clubs, winning three Champions Leagues—two with AC Milan and one with Real Madrid, making him one of the most decorated coaches in the competition. Known for his flexible tactical approach and excellent player management, Ancelotti has also triumphed in the top five European leagues, establishing a unique record in football history.

Unexpected Successes of Underestimated Teams

These teams, often seen as underdogs, have defied odds and outperformed giants of the sport through teamwork, clever strategy, and relentless determination. This showcases that in football, passion and unity can lead to extraordinary triumphs, transforming underdogs into legends and providing unforgettable moments that celebrate the very essence of sporting competition.

1. Greece, Euro 2004

Greece's victory at Euro 2004 remains one of the greatest surprises in the history of international football. Guided by Otto Rehhagel, this team defied all expectations with a tactical approach based on solid defense and effective counter-attacks. Their remarkable journey, including victories over favorite teams such as France and Portugal, not only cemented their place in history but also served as inspiration for teams considered outsiders.

2. Denmark, Euro 1992

Denmark's triumph at Euro 1992 is another uplifting example of a team defying the odds. Despite qualifying last minute due to Yugoslavia's disqualification, the Danes, led by stars like Peter Schmeichel and Brian Laudrup, displayed convincing gameplay that led them to the final victory against Germany, demonstrating that team spirit and determination can lead to success even in the most unexpected circumstances.

3. Atletico Madrid, La Liga 2013-2014

Atletico Madrid broke the duopoly of Barcelona and Real Madrid in La Liga during the 2013-2014 season under Diego Simeone's leadership. Their style of play, characterized by robust defense, collective commitment, and the ability to strike on the counter, proved that intensity and strategy could compete with pure talent, offering a valuable lesson on the importance of tactics and passion in football.

4. AS Monaco, Champions League 2016-2017

AS Monaco, with its young and dynamic squad, surprised Europe during the 2016-2017 Champions League by reaching the semifinals. Their offensive football, embodied by emerging talents like Kylian Mbappé, defied expectations and demonstrated that audacity and tactical innovation could propel a relatively modest team onto the European stage.

5. Leicester City, Premier League 2015-2016

As 5000 to 1 outsiders, Leicester achieved a unique feat by winning the Premier League in 2015-2016. Under Claudio Ranieri, the Foxes compensated for their lack of possession with direct play, lightning-fast counters, and intense pressing. The team cohesion forged by the Italian and the impeccable mindset of the players were decisive. Led by Vardy, Mahrez, and Kanté, this team of valiant warriors overturned the hierarchy.

6. South Korea, 2002 World Cup

South Korea's remarkable performance in the 2002 World Cup, where they were co-hosts, remains etched in football history. Guided by coach Guus Hiddink, the team exceeded all expectations by reaching the semi-finals, a historic achievement. By eliminating giants such as Italy and Spain, South Korea not only inspired a nation but also demonstrated that passion and tactics could transcend perceived limitations on the international stage.

7. Costa Rica - 2014 World Cup

Costa Rica was the revelation of the 2014 World Cup, advancing to the quarter-finals in a journey that captivated football fans. Overcoming the challenges of an extremely competitive group, the team exhibited exceptional resilience and unity, particularly during their memorable victory over England and their tenacious performance against the Netherlands in the quarter-finals.

8. FC Porto, 2003-2004 Champions League

FC Porto shook Europe under the management of José Mourinho in 2003-2004 by winning the Champions League against all odds. Their campaign was characterized by clever tactical play and unwavering team spirit, proving that success is not always dictated by budgets but can be achieved through strategy, passion, and cohesion.

9. Montpellier HSC, Ligue 1 2011-2012

Montpellier's Ligue 1 title in 2011-2012 remains one of the greatest feats in French football. By surpassing PSG, which had vastly superior financial resources, Montpellier demonstrated that a team's ambition and solidarity could work wonders, with key performances from players like Olivier Giroud.

10. Iceland – Euro 2016

Iceland captured the hearts of football fans at Euro 2016 by reaching the quarter-finals in what was their first major tournament. Their victory over England was particularly symbolic, showing that even the smallest nations, with team spirit and unwavering commitment, can compete against and defeat football giants, leaving a lasting legacy that inspires underestimated teams around the world.

Astonishing Football Facts

1. Most Red Cards in a Match

A match in Argentina witnessed a record 36 red cards following a massive brawl involving players, substitutes, and technical staff. This extreme incident highlights how emotions can sometimes overflow on the field, reflecting the intensity and passion that football can generate, yet also underscoring the importance of fair play and mutual respect.

2. Longest Penalty Shootout

The longest penalty shootout in history, with 48 attempts, epitomizes the incredible suspense and pressure inherent in this method of tie-breaking in football. This penalty marathon not only highlights the mental aspect of the game but also the endurance and concentration required to persevere through such an ordeal.

3. Youngest Professional

Mauricio Baldivieso's appearance in the Bolivian top division at the age of 12 is a remarkable testament to precocity and potential in sports. This exceptional record highlights the diversity of pathways in football and the importance of supporting and developing talent from an early age.

4. Coldest Football Match

A Europa League match between Astana and Sporting was played at -20°C, the coldest in the history of UEFA competitions. Playing in such extreme conditions showcases the toughness and adaptability required in sports.

5. First Female Referee in a High-Level Men's Match

Bibiana Steinhaus breaking barriers by becoming the first woman to referee in one of the top men's football leagues shows a positive evolution towards gender equality in sports. Her pioneering role in the German Bundesliga marks a significant step towards diversity and inclusion in football at all levels.

6. Highest Altitude Football Match

The record for the highest-altitude football match was set in 2007 during a game played at 6,692 meters above sea level on Mount Kilimanjaro in Tanzania. This match aimed to draw attention to the effects of climate change. Playing at such high altitude poses enormous physical challenges due to thin air, making the feat even more remarkable.

7 First FIFA Club World Championship

The establishment of the FIFA Club World Championship in 2000 marked a key milestone in club football, providing a platform for the best teams from each continent to compete. This competition has since solidified its place as the ultimate tournament to crown the best club team in the world, enriching the international football calendar.

8 First Women's World Cup

The first FIFA Women's World Cup in 1991 in China was a historic turning point. The result of a long struggle, this foundational tournament provided a global showcase for women's football. Despite limited resources, the quality of play and the enthusiasm it generated laid the groundwork for the rapid development of the sport. More than 30 years later, with 32 teams and 2 billion viewers in 2023, the progress made since the pioneers of 1991 is evident.

9 Most Capped Player

With 184 international appearances, Ahmed Hassan represents a model of longevity and dedication to football. Ahmed Hassan wore the Egypt jersey for over 16 years, from 1995 to 2012. His longevity at the highest level is remarkable. He participated in 8 Africa Cup of Nations with the Pharaohs, winning the trophy four times in 1998, 2006, 2008, and 2010. A record for titles in this competition.

10 Most Goals in a Career

Josef Bican, with over 805 career goals, embodies excellence in the art of goal-scoring. This phenomenal record not only illustrates his exceptional talent but also his ability to remain effective over a long period, providing inspiration for strikers worldwide.

11 Youngest World Cup Player

Northern Ireland's Norman Whiteside became the youngest player to participate in a World Cup in 1982 at the age of 17 years and 41 days. This record highlights the precocity and talent required to compete against the best on the global stage at such a young age..

12 Longest Goal

On March 19, 2023, in a Chilean league match, Argentine goalkeeper Leandro Requena of Cobresal scored an extraordinary goal from his own box. His powerful clearance lobbed his counterpart from Colo-Colo from an estimated distance of 101 meters. If this measurement is confirmed, Requena will erase from the records the 96.01 meters set by Tom King in 2021. A feat that reminds us that football magic can arise from anywhere, even from a goalkeeper's feet.

The Most Beautiful Goal Celebrations in Football History

Discover the most memorable and spectacular goal celebrations in the history of football. These moments of pure jubilation go beyond a simple victory gesture; they embody the passion, emotion, and sometimes even the art that permeate this sport. From spontaneous ecstasy to thought-out performances, each celebration tells a story, shares an emotion, and leaves an imprint on fans' minds.

1. Brandi Chastain - 1999 FIFA Women's World Cup

In the 1999 World Cup final, the USA and China were tied after extra time. During the penalty shootout, Brandi Chastain had the pressure of securing victory for the Americans. With a powerful left-foot strike, she beats the goalkeeper and secures the title for the USA. Overwhelmed with emotion, Chastain removes her jersey and exults on her knees in her sports bra. This powerful image has become a symbol of American women's football triumph.

2. Roger Milla - 1990 World Cup

At the 1990 World Cup, 38-year-old Roger Milla became the unexpected star for Cameroon, the first African quarterfinalist in history. His 4 goals were memorable, but it was his celebrations that captured the world's attention. After each goal, Milla would head to the corner flag to perform a joyful belly dance. These spontaneous and communicative dances became the symbol of Cameroon's epic journey and the popular fervor.

3. Peter Crouch - England, 2006

During a friendly match against Jamaica in 2006, Peter Crouch scored a hat-trick for England. After his first goal, the lanky striker surprised everyone with a completely offbeat "robot dance." With arms extended and jerky movements, Crouch performed the dance steps with a big smile, triggering laughter from the audience and his teammates. This atypical and self-deprecating celebration became his trademark, adding a touch of good-natured humor to his goals.

4. Lionel Messi - Clasico, 2017

In April 2017, Messi scored a crucial last-minute goal to secure a 3-2 victory for Barça against Real Madrid. After scoring his 500th goal in the Blaugrana jersey with surgical precision, "La Pulga" removed his jersey to proudly display it in front of the stunned Madrid supporters. A bold and provocative gesture, it instantly became iconic, celebrating a critical victory in the title race and reaffirming his dominance in the Clasico.

5. Gabriel Batistuta - Fiorentina

Gabriel Batistuta, the legendary Argentine striker for Fiorentina in the 1990s, had an iconic goal celebration. Every time he scored, "Batigol" would mimic firing a machine gun with his hands, as if "spraying" the crowd with bullets. This spectacular and slightly provocative gesture, referencing his nickname "the hitman," left a lasting impression on a generation of Fiorentina fans who saw Batistuta as a true hero.

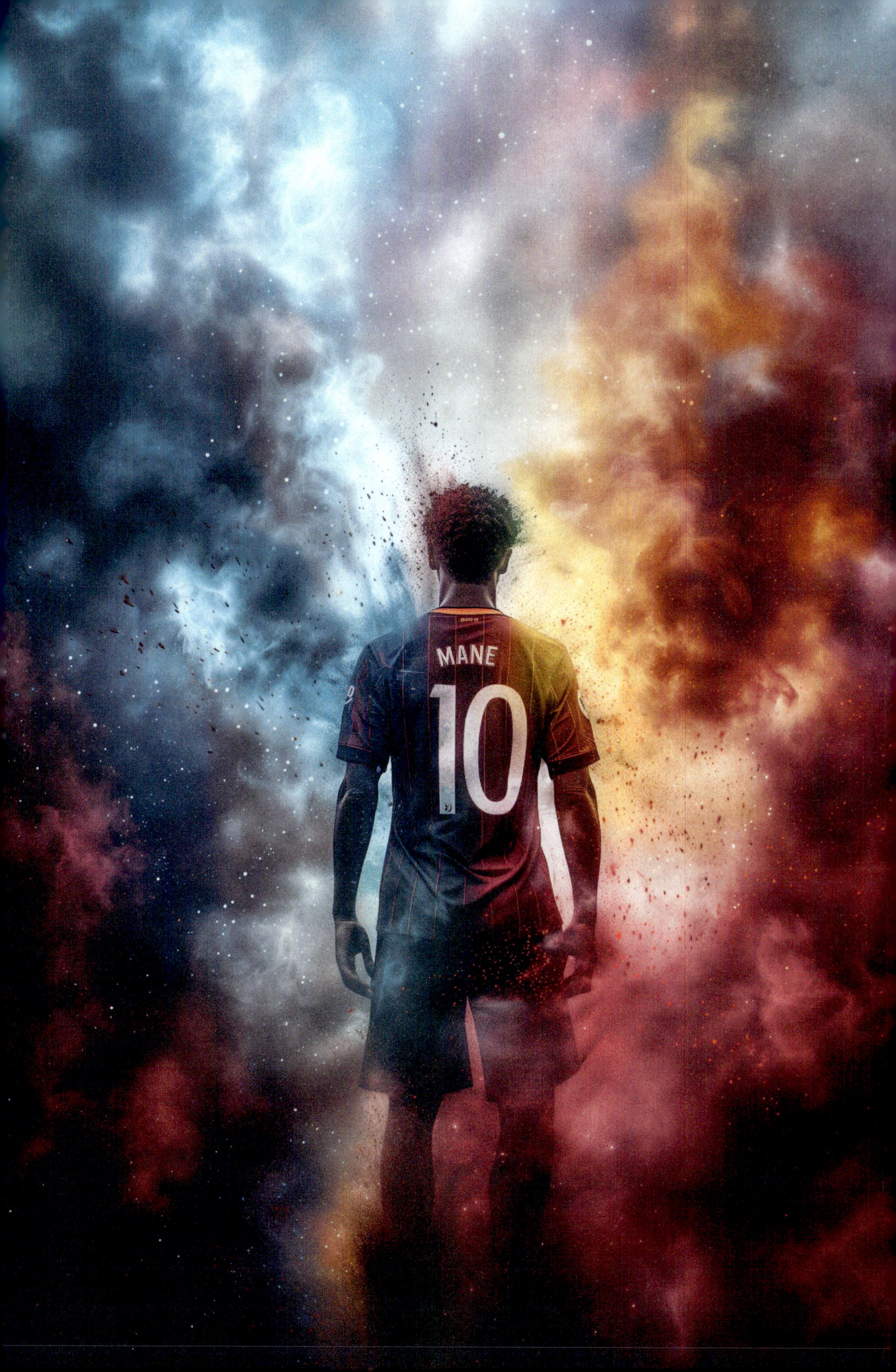
MANE
10

Memorable Technical Feats in Football

These technical exploits, a unique blend of talent, instinct, and mastery, captivate spectators and enrich the heritage of football. Whether it's a sublime control, a daring volley, or a baffling dribble, each gesture is a celebration of the art of football, demonstrating how players' ingenuity and creativity can transform an action into an unforgettable work.

1. Lionel Messi's Dribble Against Real Madrid, 2011

Lionel Messi dazzled the football world with a memorable goal against Real Madrid in the Champions League semi-final. His incredible slalom through the defense, dribbling past several players before scoring, not only showcased his exceptional talent but also his decisive impact in key moments, reinforcing his reputation as one of the greatest players of all time.

2. Zinedine Zidane's Roulette

Zinedine Zidane, with his technical mastery and elegance, perfected the roulette, a move where the player uses the ball to pivot around an opponent. His flawless execution of this gesture, particularly visible during the 2006 World Cup against Brazil, remains a testament to his class and skill, etching in minds as a symbol of his footballing genius.

3. Erik Lamela's Rabona Heel Goal

Erik Lamela scored one of the most spectacular goals in recent football history with a rabona for Tottenham, where he used his back foot to strike the ball acrobatically. This goal, with its ingenuity and technical difficulty, highlighted Lamela's ability to produce moments of pure inspiration on the field.

4. Antonín Panenka's Panenka, 1976

Antonín Panenka made this technical move famous during the 1976 European Championship final against West Germany. He executed a penalty in a daring manner, softly lobbing the ball into the center of the goal as the goalkeeper dived to the side. This move has become so iconic that it now bears his name.

5. René Higuita's Scorpion Kick

René Higuita, known for his eccentric playing style and flair for spectacle, performed a legendary save nicknamed the "scorpion kick" against England. Using his heels to flick the ball away while airborne, Higuita not only stopped the shot but also provided one of the most iconic and audacious moments in football history.

6 Juninho Pernambucano's Knuckleball Free Kick

Juninho Pernambucano, the legendary Brazilian midfielder from Olympique Lyonnais in the 2000s, revolutionized the art of the free kick. Known as "Reizinho" (the little king), he perfected the knuckleball technique: by striking the ball in a specific way, he gave it a floating, unpredictable trajectory, like a leaf swirling in the wind. Thanks to this baffling effect, Juninho scored 77 career free kicks, a record, leaving goalkeepers powerless against his strikes as precise as they were powerful.

7 Jay-Jay Okocha's Rainbow Flick

Jay-Jay Okocha, with his flamboyant playing style and technical audacity, popularized the rainbow flick, a move where the ball is played with the outside of the foot to create an unpredictable trajectory. This technique, used to surprise opponents or deliver passes and crosses, demonstrates the creativity and skill that characterize Okocha's play, making him one of the most entertaining players of his generation.

8 Lionel Messi's Chip Against Bayer Leverkusen, 2012

Lionel Messi once again demonstrated his genius when he executed a perfect chip against Bayer Leverkusen in the Champions League. This goal, where he delicately lofted the ball over the goalkeeper with surgical precision, epitomizes Messi's calmness and technical finesse, illustrating his ability to innovate and excel in critical moments.

9 Cristiano Ronaldo's Bicycle Kick Against Juventus, 2018

Cristiano Ronaldo scored one of the most spectacular goals in Champions League history with an exceptional bicycle kick against Juventus. The height and power of his strike, combined with the significance of the match, made this goal an iconic moment, showcasing Ronaldo's ability to perform high-class gestures on the most prestigious stage.

10 Paolo Di Canio's Volley Against Wimbledon, 2000

Paolo Di Canio secured his place in Premier League history with a goal of impressive technical purity against Wimbledon. His volley, executed with impeccable coordination and technique, remains an example of Di Canio's ability to produce moments of magic, consolidating his reputation as a player capable of beautiful and effective gestures.

Well-Kept Secrets

1. Anfield's Secret Grass Recipe

Anfield employs a unique combination of grass types and maintenance techniques, but the exact details remain a closely guarded secret of Liverpool FC. This specific recipe helps the pitch withstand harsh weather and intense play, contributing to Anfield's reputation as one of the most prestigious football grounds in the world.

2. Hidden Messages in FC Barcelona's Jerseys

The 2020-2021 FC Barcelona jerseys paid homage to the Eixample, an emblematic district of the city. The home jersey featured a blue and garnet checkerboard pattern reminiscent of the district's grid-like urban plan designed by Ildefons Cerdà, highlighting the connection between the club and the city. The black away jersey also featured motifs evoking the Eixample, a bold choice reinforcing the Catalan identity of Barça beyond mere aesthetics.

3. The Hidden Role of Psychologists in Top Teams

Manchester United pioneered the integration of psychologist Bill Beswick into its staff in 1999. Focusing on mental preparation, Beswick helped players develop a fighter mentality to manage pressure. His approach, complementing Ferguson's strategies, contributed to the Red Devils' successes, notably assisting Roy Keane and Gary Neville through periods of doubt. His tenure paved the way for the widespread adoption of mental coaches in elite football.

4. Unusual Clauses in Players' Contracts

When Stefan Schwarz signed with Sunderland in 1999, an unusual clause was added to his contract prohibiting space travel, due to fears one of his sponsors might send him to space. This unique clause highlights the breadth of considerations in modern contract negotiations.

5. Clubs' Secret Recruitment Techniques

FC Porto is renowned for its extensive scouting network and ability to discover unknown talents. The club uses advanced analysis software and scouts who attend hundreds of matches, sometimes incognito, to identify future stars. The precise details of these methods remain a competitive advantage for the club.

6. Players' Pre-Match Rituals

Lionel Messi, like many footballers, has his own pre-match rituals. He is often the last player to enter the pitch, always stepping with his right foot first. This simple yet consistent routine appears to be part of his mental preparation. Messi has also been seen making religious gestures like crossing himself before stepping onto the field, a ritual shared by many players.

7 Hidden Training of Top-Level Referees

Top-level referees, such as those in the Premier League or FIFA, undergo extensive training that includes video simulations and psychological tests to enhance their decision-making and stress management. Details of these programs are rarely disclosed, emphasizing the importance of mental and technical preparation in refereeing.

8 Secret Conversations via Referees' Microphones

During matches, referees exchange crucial information via microphones, discussions that remain confidential. These exchanges help maintain consistency and fairness in decisions, but their exact content remains a mystery to spectators and teams alike.

9 Coaches' Coded Game Plans

Coaches like Pep Guardiola or Jürgen Klopp might use codes or signals to convey instructions without being understood by opponents. These coded tactics allow for rapid strategic shifts without drawing the attention of the opposition.

10 Strict Rules for Handling the World Cup Trophy

Aside from the official award ceremony and the return to the home country, only former World Cup champions and heads of state are allowed to touch the World Cup, highlighting the sacred status of the trophy.

11 The Science Behind Penalty Shootouts

Teams secretly analyze shooters' and goalkeepers' preferences for penalty shootouts, relying on statistical data to maximize success chances. Studying habits can influence the selection of shooters and the strategy of goalkeepers during these critical moments.

12 Ultra-Secret Medical Monitoring of Players

Football clubs maintain strict confidentiality on medical data and performance analytics of their players. This includes information on physical fitness, injury risks, and recovery plans, essential for keeping athletes in optimal condition while preserving a competitive edge.

Humanitarian and Charitable Impact of Football Stars

Discover the extraordinary impact and humanitarian contributions of football stars around the world. These players not only shine on the field; they also use their influence and resources to initiate positive changes, support charitable causes, and improve lives beyond the stadiums.

1. Didier Drogba and Peace in Ivory Coast (2007)

In 2007, after qualifying Ivory Coast for the World Cup, Didier Drogba made an impassioned plea for the end of the civil war, which led to a ceasefire. His intervention was crucial for the peaceful conduct of elections. Drogba used his fame to unite his country, becoming a symbol of peace and significantly contributing to national reconciliation.

2. Juan Mata and the Common Goal Project (Launched in 2017)

Juan Mata initiated Common Goal in 2017, inviting football professionals to donate 1% of their salaries to community and charitable football projects worldwide. This initiative has attracted dozens of players and coaches, generating significant financial support for underprivileged communities and demonstrating the collective impact of football on social causes.

3. Lionel Messi and the Leo Messi Foundation (Established in 2007)

Since its establishment, the Leo Messi Foundation has contributed to various social and health projects, including funding the construction of pediatric centers in Argentina, renovating hospitals, and supporting children's education. The foundation has had a global impact, improving the lives of thousands of children and demonstrating Messi's commitment to humanitarian causes.

4. Sadio Mané and His Contributions to Senegal

Senegalese striker Sadio Mané has invested heavily in his hometown of Bambali. He funded the construction of a school, estimated at about 250,000 euros, and a hospital for 530,000 euros, inaugurated in 2021. These vital infrastructures have transformed the daily lives of residents, demonstrating the direct impact a player can have on their community.

5. Cristiano Ronaldo and His Generous Donations

Cristiano Ronaldo is known for his generosity, including a donation of 1.5 million euros to fund meals for Palestinian children in 2012 and another donation of 600,000 euros to a children's hospital in Portugal in 2016. He also contributed to the fight against COVID-19 by funding intensive care units in Portuguese hospitals in 2020.

6. Marcus Rashford and His Campaign Against Child Hunger

In 2020, English forward Marcus Rashford led an influential campaign to extend the free meal program in the UK, impacting the government's decision to provide food vouchers during school holidays. His petition gathered over one million signatures, highlighting the issue of child food security and contributing to a policy change beneficial to millions of families.

7. Nwankwo Kanu and the Kanu Heart Foundation (Launched in 2000)

After undergoing heart surgery himself, former Nigerian footballer Nwankwo Kanu founded the Kanu Heart Foundation to aid African children suffering from heart diseases. The foundation has funded vital surgical operations for over 500 children to date. Kanu has used his fame to raise awareness and funds, showing a deep commitment to distressed children in Africa.

8. Mesut Özil and His Support for Children's Surgeries (2014 World Cup)

Mesut Özil used his earnings from the 2014 World Cup to fund surgeries for 23 Brazilian children in need. The cost of these surgeries amounted to about 240,000 euros. Özil has regularly engaged in charitable initiatives, but this particular act highlighted his desire to have a tangible positive impact on the lives of underprivileged children.

9. Kylian Mbappé's Philanthropic Commitment (Since 2018)

Since 2018, Kylian Mbappé has been making generous gestures towards charitable causes. He donated his 2018 World Cup earnings to an organization for hospitalized children and made contributions to aid the underprivileged during the Covid-19 crisis. Mbappé's charitable efforts primarily focus on supporting the most vulnerable, making him a model of altruism.

10. David Beckham and His Work with UNICEF (Since 2005)

Engaged with UNICEF for over a decade, David Beckham launched the 7 Fund in 2015 to protect and support children worldwide. Through this initiative, Beckham aims to raise funds and awareness about major issues affecting children, including violence, malnutrition, and lack of education. His ongoing commitment demonstrates the positive influence footballers can have beyond the field.

11 Iker Casillas and the Iker Casillas Foundation

The iconic former goalkeeper of Real Madrid and the Spanish national team established his foundation to promote education and sports among youth, as well as support various health projects. The foundation particularly focuses on underprivileged children, offering opportunities and resources for their development and well-being.

12 Andrés Iniesta and His Support for Victims of the 2011 Japan Earthquake

Andrés Iniesta profoundly touched hearts by offering support to the victims of the 2011 earthquake and tsunami in Japan. Known for his commitment, he helped rebuild schools and support children affected by the disaster, using his popularity to raise awareness and encourage donations, reflecting his empathy and commitment to distressed communities.

13 Samuel Eto'o and His Humanitarian Efforts in Africa (Since the 2000s)

Former Cameroonian striker Samuel Eto'o has played a key role in various charitable initiatives in Africa, including contributing to the construction of schools and hospitals. His foundation, established in the mid-2000s, has supported thousands of children and families by providing scholarships, healthcare, and educational opportunities, demonstrating his commitment to improving living conditions on his native continent.

14 Michael Essien and His Action Against the Ebola Virus (2014)

In 2014, Ghanaian footballer Michael Essien launched a commendable initiative to combat the Ebola epidemic in West Africa. With a personal contribution of $500,000, he actively participated in efforts to contain the disease and support affected people. Additionally, he used his fame to raise awareness of this cause.

15 Megan Rapinoe and Her Activism for Gender Equality and LGBTQ+ Rights (Active since the 2010s)

American star Megan Rapinoe is not only known for her on-field performances but also for her committed activism. She has been a powerful voice for gender equality in sports, social justice, and LGBTQ+ rights, using her visibility to influence public debate and support marginalized communities, proving that her legacy extends far beyond athletic achievements.

Speed Records on the Field

These speed records on the field highlight the impressive combination of power, endurance, and agility, showcasing athletes who use their exceptional speed to change the course of games. Whether through breathtaking sprints or lightning-fast accelerations, these moments captivate fans and demonstrate how speed, one of the most thrilling qualities in sports, can be a decisive asset in a player's arsenal.

1. Kylian Mbappé against Argentina, 2018 World Cup

Kylian Mbappé captured global attention during the 2018 World Cup with a dazzling sprint against Argentina, where his prodigious speed was highlighted. Covering 70 meters in 7.3 seconds to earn a penalty, his acceleration was crucial in France's victory, demonstrating not only his individual talent but also his significant impact at a key moment in the tournament.

2. Achraf Hakimi, Borussia Dortmund vs. Union Berlin, Bundesliga 2020

During his tenure at Borussia Dortmund, Achraf Hakimi impressed with his speed on the field, recording a top speed of 36.48 km/h against Union Berlin. This performance not only underscored his status as one of the world's fastest players but also illustrated his crucial role in his team's offensive dynamics.

3. Alphonso Davies, FC Bayern Munich vs. Werder Bremen, Bundesliga 2020

On June 16, 2020, in a match against Werder Bremen, Alphonso Davies was clocked at 36.51 km/h, setting a new Bundesliga speed record. His phenomenal speed, combined with his technique and game vision, makes him one of the most formidable and promising defenders in global football.

4. Adama Traoré

Adama Traoré is a force of nature. The Spanish winger for Wolverhampton is among the fastest players in the world, capable of reaching speeds up to 37.8 km/h. Traoré poses a true challenge for opposing defenders, combining blistering acceleration with impressive physical strength, making him one of the most dynamic wingers in the Premier League.

5. Theo Walcott, Arsenal vs. Liverpool, Premier League 2008

Theo Walcott showcased his lightning speed during a match against Liverpool in 2008, where he made a memorable sprint along the length of the field, bypassing several opponents before delivering a decisive pass. This moment was emblematic of his career, highlighting his speed as one of his major assets on the field.

Outstanding Goalkeeper Performances

These goalkeepers, true bulwarks for their teams, have performed feats that go far beyond simple saves. From astonishing reflex saves to crucial interventions at critical moments, these performances illustrate the art of goalkeeping at its peak.

1 Lev Yashin at the 1966 World Cup

Lev Yashin, known as "The Black Spider," made history at the 1966 World Cup with his exceptional performances. His playing style, combining impressive reflex saves and the ability to organize the defense, not only led the Soviet Union to the semi-finals but also revolutionized the role of the goalkeeper, establishing Yashin as one of the greatest goalkeepers of all time.

2 Gordon Banks against Brazil in 1970

During the 1970 World Cup, English goalkeeper Gordon Banks made what is considered the greatest save in history. From Jairzinho's cross, Pelé headed a powerful and diving shot that seemed unstoppable. However, Banks incredibly stretched to his right to turn the ball over the bar with a one-handed save. A physics-defying gesture that left Pelé incredulous and has become a legendary moment in football history.

3 Iker Casillas in the 2010 World Cup

Iker Casillas, captain of Spain, played a decisive role in their historic 2010 World Cup victory. His key interventions, especially in the final against the Netherlands, were crucial. The save against Robben remains a highlight of his career, symbolizing his reactivity and leadership, fundamental in Spain's success.

4 Manuel Neuer at the 2014 World Cup

Manuel Neuer redefined the goalkeeper position at the 2014 World Cup with his unique abilities as a "sweeper-keeper." His performances against Algeria and Argentina showcased his mastery of the game, combining decisive saves with a reassuring presence outside his line, significantly contributing to Germany's triumph.

5 Gianluigi Buffon in the 2006 World Cup Final

Gianluigi Buffon was a pillar for Italy throughout the 2006 World Cup, culminating with his performance in the final against France. His saves, particularly against Zidane, were crucial in keeping Italy in the game, leading to their victory in the penalty shootout. Buffon's consistency and expertise were invaluable assets for Italy in their quest for the world title.

6. Tim Howard at the 2014 World Cup against Belgium

Tim Howard put on a legendary performance at the 2014 World Cup against Belgium, with 15 saves, a record in World Cup history. His extraordinary showing captivated football fans worldwide, making him a symbol of determination and excellence, even though the United States was eliminated after the match.

7. Peter Schmeichel in the 1999 Champions League Final

Peter Schmeichel was instrumental for Manchester United in the 1999 Champions League final, contributing to his team's victory against Bayern Munich. His decisive saves and imposing presence played a key role in Manchester United's success, who scored two late goals to win the title. This performance helped Manchester United complete a historic treble and cemented Schmeichel's status among the greatest goalkeepers of all time.

8. Keylor Navas during the 2017-2018 Champions League

Keylor Navas was a key factor in Real Madrid's Champions League success, especially during the 2017-2018 campaign. His performances, particularly against Bayern Munich and Juventus, demonstrated his ability to make crucial saves at critical moments, playing a central role in Real Madrid's European title conquest.

9. Claudio Bravo in the 2016 Copa America Final

Claudio Bravo was crucial in Chile's success at the 2016 Copa America, particularly in the final against Argentina. His decisive saves during the penalty shootout enabled Chile to lift the trophy, highlighting his ability to be decisive in the tensest moments.

10. David de Gea against Arsenal, Premier League 2017

David de Gea had a memorable performance against Arsenal in 2017, making 14 saves, tying the Premier League record for most saves in a match. His spectacular interventions were crucial for Manchester United, allowing his team to secure a 3-1 victory in a match where the Spanish goalkeeper was the undisputed protagonist.

Achievements of Disabled Players

These remarkable athletes, faced with unique challenges, have shown resilience, talent, and passion that inspire and move people. Their remarkable journeys on the field offer lessons in courage, perseverance, and commitment, proving that football is truly an inclusive sport that celebrates diversity and human excellence.

1. Nico Calabria - Overhead Scissor Kick Despite Amputation

In 2012, Nico Calabria, an American high school student amputated from the right leg, scored an incredible goal during a match with his team. On a corner, he rose and performed a scissor kick with surgical precision, sending the ball into the top corner. The video of this feat went viral, accumulating over 1.7 million views on YouTube. A technically challenging move that highlighted the talent and determination of this extraordinary player.

2. Héctor Rodas - A Remarkable Career Despite a Disability

Héctor Rodas, a Spanish defender born without a left leg below the knee, achieved an unprecedented feat in professional football. Despite his disability, he played for 10 seasons in Spain's third division against able-bodied players. Playing with a prosthesis, Rodas demonstrated exceptional determination and endurance to establish himself at this level. An inspiring example that pushes boundaries and proves that overcoming oneself can lead to extraordinary achievements on the football field.

3. Shea Cowart - Historic Triple at the 2012 Paralympic Games

Shea Cowart, a member of the U.S. Paralympic football team, accomplished a resounding feat during the final at the London 2012 Games. Amputated below both knees due to meningitis at the age of 6, Cowart overcame her disability to become a top athlete. In this final, she scored a decisive hat-trick that greatly contributed to the United States' victory. An exceptional performance that commands respect.

4. Dave Clarke - Legend of English Blind Football

Dave Clarke, an English striker who is blind, is a legend in blind football (football 5-a-side). Despite his disability, he scored 128 goals in 144 appearances for Great Britain, making him the all-time top scorer. Thanks to his innate goal-scoring sense and exceptional technique, Clarke has greatly contributed to British successes in this sport, including winning a silver medal at the 2008 Paralympics. An inspiring example of self-improvement and talent.

5. Yannick Villedieu - Supreme Distinction in 7-a-side Football

Yannick Villedieu, a French goalkeeper with cerebral palsy, excelled with the French 7-a-side football team during the 2015 World Cup. Despite his disability affecting his motor skills, Villedieu performed wonders in the French goal throughout the tournament. His reflexes, positioning, and decisive saves earned him the title of the best goalkeeper of the competition, a well-deserved accolade for this exceptional player who pushes the limits.

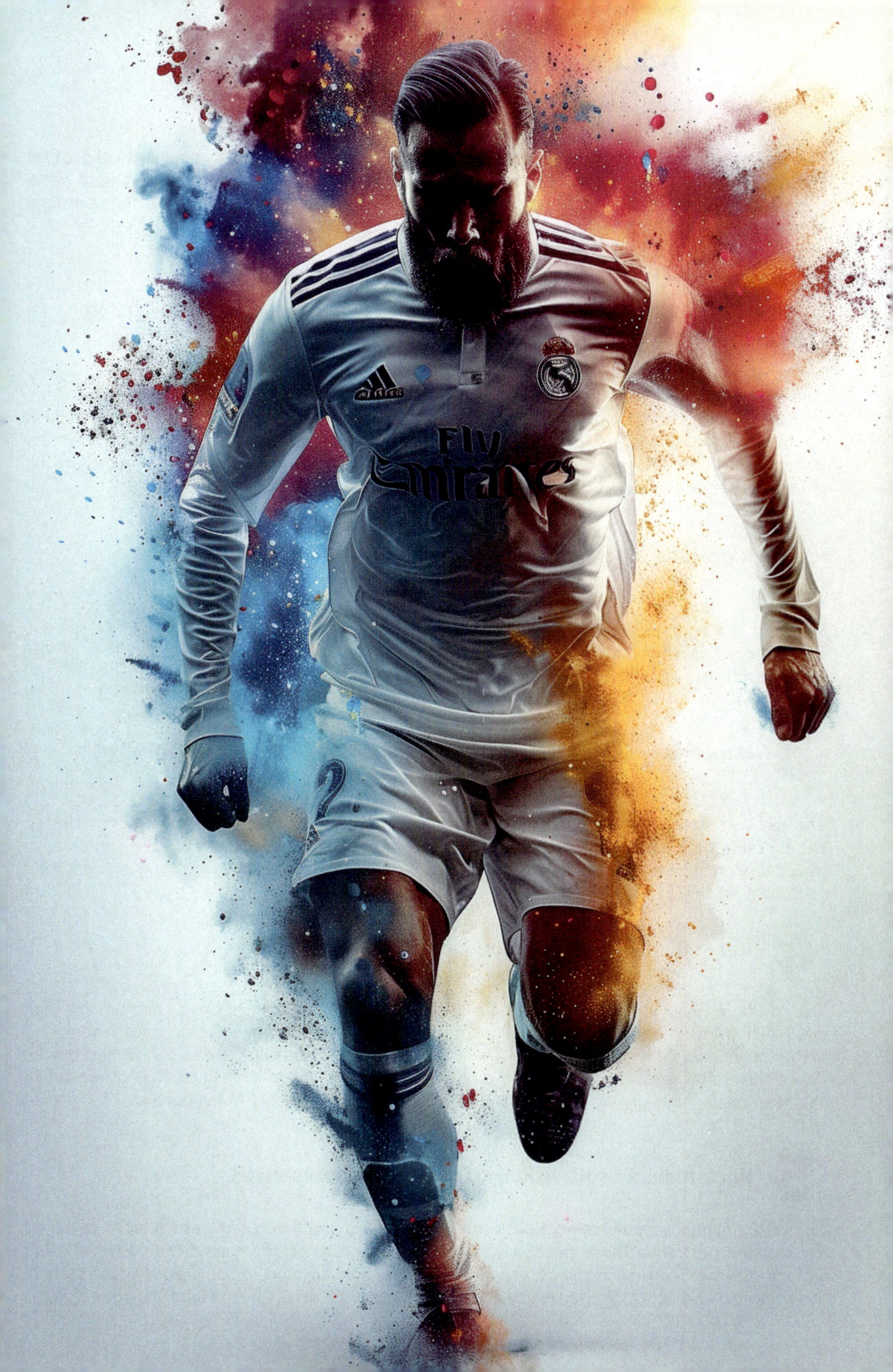
Fly

Achievements in Derbies and Rivalries

These encounters are the stage for historic clashes, overflowing passions, and often transcendental stakes. The achievements in these emblematic duels are not just victories or remarkable individual performances, but moments etched in collective memory, where honor, pride, and sometimes even a community's identity are at stake.

1. The North London Derby - Harry Kane (Tottenham vs Arsenal, 2016)

In one of the most electrifying North London derbies, Tottenham Hotspur's striker Harry Kane scored a memorable goal against Arsenal. From a particularly difficult angle, Kane unleashed a shot that found the back of the net, demonstrating not only his surgical precision but also his knack for rising to the occasion. This goal was not only spectacular for its technique but also played a crucial role in Tottenham's victory, reinforcing their stance in one of the most passionate rivalries in English football.

2. Barcelona 5-0 Real Madrid (2010)

In one of the most memorable Clásicos, FC Barcelona crushed Real Madrid 5-0 at Camp Nou. This victory not only highlighted Barça's superiority at that time but also marked one of the heaviest defeats of Real Madrid in the history of this rivalry.

3. Manchester City vs Manchester United, Premier League 2011-2012

The decisive match of the 2011-2012 season saw Manchester City beat Manchester United 1-0, a result that not only decided the Premier League title but also symbolized the shift in power in Manchester football. Vincent Kompany's goal was a pivotal moment, marking City's rise and a turning point in their rivalry with United.

4. Inter Milan vs AC Milan, Serie A 2005

The 2005 Milan derby, a Champions League quarter-final return leg, was marked by high emotional intensity, typical of clashes between Inter and AC Milan. AC Milan was leading 1-0 with a goal from Andriy Shevchenko when the match was interrupted and abandoned due to flares thrown by fans. UEFA awarded a forfeit victory to AC Milan, which thus advanced to the semi-finals, highlighting the passion and pride characteristic of Milan derbies.

5. Boca Juniors vs River Plate, Copa Libertadores 2018

The 2018 Copa Libertadores final between Boca Juniors and River Plate was a historic event, marking the first time these fierce rivals met at this stage of the competition. River Plate's victory, after extra time in the return match, was an epic moment in South American football, underscoring the depth of the rivalry and the passion that drives both clubs and their fans.

6 Arsenal vs Tottenham, Premier League 2004

Arsenal's 2003-2004 season went down in history with their match against Tottenham, where they secured the Premier League title while remaining undefeated throughout the season, earning them the nickname "The Invincibles". The 2-2 draw at White Hart Lane was an iconic moment, celebrating Arsenal's supremacy in English football and adding a special intensity to the North London rivalry.

7 Borussia Dortmund vs Schalke 04, Bundesliga 2017

The 2017 Ruhr derby between Dortmund and Schalke turned out to be an emotional rollercoaster. Dortmund, leading 4-0 at halftime, witnessed Schalke make a remarkable comeback to finish the game 4-4. This match has become a reference point for comebacks in football and intensified the rivalry between the two clubs.

8 Celtic vs Rangers, Scottish Premiership 1999

Celtic's resounding 5-1 victory over Rangers in 1999 remains a highlight in the rivalry between the two Glasgow clubs. This match not only solidified Celtic's dominance that season but also highlighted the passion and intensity of the Glasgow derby, one of the most fervent in the world.

9 FC Barcelona vs Espanyol, La Liga 2007

The draw between FC Barcelona and Espanyol in 2007 is a memorable moment in the Barcelona rivalry. Espanyol, by snatching a 2-2 draw, played a pivotal role in the title race, indirectly preventing Barça from winning La Liga, which added an extra layer of tension between the two teams.

10 Olympique de Marseille vs Paris Saint-Germain, Ligue 1 2011

Olympique de Marseille's 3-0 triumph over PSG in 2011 was a significant moment in their rivalry. This victory not only fueled the animosity between the two most followed clubs in France but also gave Marseille fans a reason to celebrate against their long-standing adversary, highlighting the intensity and passion that characterize the clashes between OM and PSG.

11 Liverpool vs Everton, Premier League 2020

In the 2020 Merseyside derby, Liverpool displayed their dominance by defeating Everton 5-2. This victory wasn't just a testament to Liverpool's supremacy in the city but also reflected their dominance in that season's Premier League. The rivalry between Liverpool and Everton, one of the oldest and most passionate in English football, was once again highlighted in this memorable match.

12 AS Roma vs Lazio, Serie A 2017

The 2017 Rome derby saw AS Roma triumph over Lazio with a 3-1 scoreline, a match fraught with emotion and crucial for European competition qualifications. The victory not only solidified Roma's position but also gave their fans significant bragging rights, illustrating the intensity and passion that define this historic derby of Italy's capital.

13 Atlético Madrid vs Real Madrid, Champions League 2016

The 2016 Champions League final between Atlético and Real Madrid was a pivotal moment in Madrid's football rivalry. Despite losing in a penalty shootout, Atlético demonstrated their grit and capability to compete at the highest level, showcasing the fierce rivalry that drives both clubs from Spain's capital.

14 Galatasaray vs Fenerbahçe, Süper Lig 2012

The 2012 match between Galatasaray and Fenerbahçe was a significant highlight in the Süper Lig, with Galatasaray securing a 3-2 victory at the home of their eternal rivals. This result was crucial for Galatasaray's title win that season, exacerbating the rivalry between Istanbul's two most popular clubs and underlining the importance of this derby in Turkish football.

15 Boca Juniors vs River Plate, Superliga Argentina 2018

The Argentine Superclásico between Boca Juniors and River Plate in 2018 ended with a 2-0 victory for Boca, a match that bolstered the legendary rivalry between the two clubs. This win was particularly symbolic, occurring before their historic meeting in the Copa Libertadores final, adding an extra layer of intensity to the competition between these two giants of Argentine football.

Transfer Records and Economic Impacts

These transfers are not just mere player movements; they represent strategic statements of intent by clubs, investments aimed at transforming their sporting and commercial futures. Each transfer record underscores the evolution of the market and reflects the economic dynamics that drive modern football.

1. Neymar, from Barcelona to Paris Saint-Germain in 2017

Neymar's transfer to PSG for a record amount of 222 million euros not only shook the football world but also highlighted the Parisian club's ambition to establish itself as a dominant force in Europe. This transfer marked a turning point, showing PSG's desire to attract world-class talent and compete at the highest level.

2. Kylian Mbappé, from Monaco to Paris Saint-Germain in 2018

Kylian Mbappé's move to PSG, following a loan turned into a permanent transfer for about 180 million euros, confirmed the club's strategy to invest in young prodigies. Mbappé, one of the most promising talents of his generation, has strengthened the Parisian attack, solidifying PSG's European ambitions.

3. Philippe Coutinho, from Liverpool to FC Barcelona in 2018

The transfer of Philippe Coutinho to FC Barcelona for 160 million euros was one of the most expensive in football history. Barcelona sought to fill the void left by Neymar and to add creativity to its midfield, placing high expectations on the Brazilian's shoulders.

4. João Félix, from Benfica to Atlético de Madrid in 2019

Atlético de Madrid's acquisition of João Félix for 126 million euros was a record investment for the club, demonstrating their commitment to recruiting young talents with high potential. Félix, considered one of the brightest prospects in European football, was seen as a central piece of Atlético's sporting project.

5. Paul Pogba, from Juventus to Manchester United in 2016

Paul Pogba's transfer to Manchester United for 105 million euros not only broke the world record at the time but also symbolized United's return to the upper echelons of global football. This transfer was meant to mark the beginning of a new era at Old Trafford, with Pogba at the heart of the team's project.

Apex of Historic Clubs

This exploration traces the glorious periods when these clubs were not just teams, but symbols of excellence, success, and innovation. Whether through their dominance on the national or international stage, their contributions to the tactical development of the game, or their ability to captivate fans with memorable performances, these clubs have written vibrant chapters in football history, defining eras that continue to inspire admiration and nostalgia.

1. Real Madrid, Late 1950s

Real Madrid in the 1950s is often regarded as one of the greatest teams of all time, having set a standard of excellence with five consecutive European Champion Clubs' Cup victories. Players like Alfredo Di Stefano and Ferenc Puskas were central to this dominance, making history with their talent and ability to revolutionize the game, leaving a legacy that continues to influence the club today.

2. Ajax Amsterdam, Early 1970s

Ajax Amsterdam revolutionized global football in the early 1970s with the introduction of "Total Football." Under the guidance of Rinus Michels and featuring stars like Johan Cruyff, Ajax dominated Europe by winning three consecutive European Cups. Their style of play, characterized by fluidity, interchangeability of positions, and ball possession, has left an indelible imprint on the sport.

3. AC Milan, Late 1980s and Early 1990s

AC Milan during this period, under the aegis of Arrigo Sacchi and later Fabio Capello, established a standard of excellence with its innovative style of play and success in Europe. Milan won several Champions League titles and Serie A championships, marking an era with a team that combined talent, tactical discipline, and innovation.

4. FC Barcelona, Early 2010s

FC Barcelona, under the leadership of Pep Guardiola, defined an era with its possession-based and attacking play, known as tiki-taka, which captivated the football world. With players like Messi, Xavi, and Iniesta, Barça not only dominated Europe but also provided a spectacle that redefined expectations for team play and football strategy.

5. Manchester United, Late 1990s and Early 2000s

Under Sir Alex Ferguson, Manchester United experienced a golden era, characterized by Champions League victories in 1999 and 2008, as well as numerous Premier League titles. Known for its dynamic style of play and ability to excel in key moments, the team was one of the dominant forces in global football, marking an era with its success and engaging style of play.

6 Liverpool, Late 1970s to Early 1980s

Liverpool, under the management of Bob Paisley and Joe Fagan, established a hegemony in England and Europe, winning the European Cup four times and several English league titles during this period. Their football, based on solid defensive organization and offensive efficiency, made Liverpool one of the most feared and respected teams of the era, leaving a lasting legacy in football history.

7 Bayern Munich, Mid-1970s

The Bayern Munich of this era, with icons like Franz Beckenbauer, Gerd Müller, and Sepp Maier, dominated European football by winning the European Champion Clubs' Cup three times consecutively. This golden period not only underscored Bayern's supremacy on the continent but also laid the foundations of its reputation as a European giant.

8 Inter Milan, Mid-1960s

Under Helenio Herrera, Inter Milan epitomized Italian football excellence, winning two European Champion Clubs' Cups and several Serie A titles thanks to the "catenaccio" strategy. This defensive approach, combined with sharp counter-attacks, established Inter as a major force in 1960s football.

9 Juventus, Late 1990s

Juventus marked the 1990s by reaching three Champions League finals and winning the title in 1996. Talents like Del Piero and Zidane were at the heart of this team that dominated the Italian and European scenes, demonstrating a quality of play that captivated global football fans.

10 FC Porto, Early 2000s

With José Mourinho at the helm, FC Porto experienced one of the most glorious periods in its history, winning the Champions League in 2004 after securing the UEFA Cup the previous year. This era saw Porto establish itself as a dominant force in Portugal and make a name for itself on the European stage with pragmatic yet captivating football.

Crushing Victories and Match Dominations

Dive into moments where football transcends mere competition to enter the realm of the extraordinary, with crushing victories and match dominations that define the pinnacle of a team's success. These encounters, far from being mere matches, transform into displays of power, where tactics, talent, and determination combine to create unforgettable spectacles.

1. Manchester United vs. Arsenal, Premier League 2011

Manchester United delivered one of its most memorable performances by crushing Arsenal 8-2 at Old Trafford. With a hat-trick from Wayne Rooney and significant contributions from Ashley Young, United demonstrated relentless offensive power, marking this match as a historic moment in the rivalry between the two clubs, while exposing Arsenal's vulnerabilities at that time.

2. Germany vs. Brazil, 2014 World Cup Semi-final

The 2014 World Cup semi-final between Germany and Brazil will remain in history as one of the most dominant displays in football. With a 7-1 victory, including five goals in just 29 minutes, Germany not only humiliated Brazil on its home soil but also displayed crushing efficiency and coordination, while seeing Miroslav Klose become the all-time top scorer in World Cup history.

3. Bayern Munich vs. Barcelona, 2020 Champions League Quarter-final

Bayern Munich dominated FC Barcelona with a staggering score of 8-2 in a unique Champions League quarter-final match in 2020. This encounter, marked by outstanding performances from players like Thomas Müller and Philippe Coutinho, not only highlighted Bayern's superiority but also exposed Barça's structural and tactical weaknesses at that time.

4. Real Madrid vs. Malmo, 2015 Champions League Group Stage

Real Madrid inflicted a resounding 8-0 defeat on Malmo, with Cristiano Ronaldo setting a record by scoring 11 goals in the group stage of the competition. With a hat-trick from Karim Benzema, this match demonstrated the strength and depth of the Madrid squad, underlining their status as title contenders.

5. Brazil vs. Italy, 1970 World Cup Final

The 1970 World Cup final saw Brazil deliver a football masterclass, beating Italy 4-1. Brazil's captivating play, marked by legendary performances from Pelé, Jairzinho, Gérson, and an unforgettable goal by Carlos Alberto, cemented this Brazilian team as one of the greatest of all time, showcasing football that combines beauty, creativity, and efficiency.

6. Liverpool vs. Besiktas, Champions League 2007-2008

Liverpool delivered a remarkable performance by crushing Besiktas 8-0 at Anfield during the 2007-2008 Champions League. With a hat-trick by Yossi Benayoun, Liverpool not only demonstrated its offensive power but also made history in the competition by the magnitude of its victory, reflecting the quality and depth of its squad.

7. Spain vs. Tahiti, Confederations Cup 2013

Spain established its superiority by defeating Tahiti 10-0 during the 2013 Confederations Cup. Fernando Torres, with four goals, led Spain in a match that highlighted the difference in caliber between the two teams, emphasizing the Spanish technical and tactical proficiency.

8. Arbroath vs. Bon Accord (36-0, 1885)

Arbroath demolished Bon Accord 36-0 in a Scottish Cup match. This score remains the largest victory in professional football history. Arbroath's John Petrie scored 13 goals that day, a single-match individual record that still stands. Bon Accord had only 9 players at kickoff and had to recruit spectators to complete the team. The referee even disallowed 7 additional goals for Arbroath.

9. Manchester City vs. Burton Albion, English League Cup 2018-2019

Manchester City showcased its strength in the League Cup semi-final by defeating Burton Albion 9-0. Gabriel Jesus, with four goals, was central to this display, highlighting the depth and quality of City's squad against an clearly overwhelmed Burton team.

10. Australia vs. American Samoa, 2002 World Cup Qualifiers

Australia set a world record during the 2002 World Cup qualifiers by defeating American Samoa 31-0. Archie Thompson, with 13 goals, delivered a historic performance, highlighting the immense gap in level between the two teams and marking this match as a unique moment in international football history.

Triumphant Injury Comebacks

These stories of determination recount the journeys of players who overcame seemingly insurmountable obstacles to return stronger to the field. Each story is a testament to strength, willpower, and commitment to recovery.

1. Neymar Jr. (Paris Saint-Germain, 2018)

Neymar, one of the world's top football stars, suffered a metatarsal injury in February 2018, jeopardizing his participation in the World Cup in Russia. After undergoing surgery and an intensive rehabilitation process, Neymar made an impressive return to the field in June 2018, just in time to represent Brazil at the World Cup. Despite immense pressure and doubts about his physical condition, he showcased his exceptional talent and determination, significantly contributing to the Brazilian team's performance, which reached the quarter-finals.

2. Zlatan Ibrahimović (Manchester United, 2017)

At 35, Zlatan Ibrahimović suffered a severe anterior cruciate ligament injury in April 2017, an injury many would have considered career-ending, especially at that age. However, his spectacular comeback in November 2017 astounded the football world. His rehabilitation, mental strength, and determination not only enabled a swift return but also proved he remained a formidable force, scoring goals and influencing younger players at Manchester United.

3. Aaron Ramsey (Arsenal, 2010)

Aaron Ramsey's promising career was abruptly halted in February 2010 when a horrific collision led to an open fracture of his leg. The road to recovery was far from straightforward for the Welsh midfielder, involving multiple surgeries and a lengthy rehabilitation process. Yet, in less than a year, Ramsey made his triumphant return, not only reclaiming his place in the Arsenal team but also refining his skills to become one of the club's most influential players.

4. Roberto Baggio (Italy, 1994 World Cup)

Roberto Baggio, one of the most talented footballers of his generation, had a mixed year in 1994. After a season plagued by injuries, Baggio led Italy to the World Cup final in the United States, scoring five goals along the way. Despite ongoing pain and the burden of expectations, he was pivotal in each match, driving his team to the final against Brazil. His performance throughout the tournament, despite a recurring thigh injury, remains a testament to his resilience and impact on the field, although the final is often remembered for his missed penalty.

5. Ruud van Nistelrooy (Manchester United, 2001)

Dutch striker Ruud van Nistelrooy saw his transfer to Manchester United delayed by a year due to a severe knee injury in 2000. After surgery and a prolonged rehabilitation period, van Nistelrooy joined United in 2001 and immediately made a significant impact, scoring 23 goals in 32 Premier League appearances in his debut season.

6. Luke Shaw (Manchester United, 2015)

After sustaining a double leg fracture in September 2015 during a Champions League match against PSV Eindhoven, Luke Shaw faced a long recovery period. The severity of the injury cast doubts over his return to top-level football. However, Shaw made an impressive comeback, not only fighting to regain his physical form but also overcoming the psychological hurdles associated with such an injury.

7. Eduardo da Silva (Arsenal, 2008)

Brazilian-Croatian striker Eduardo da Silva suffered an open leg fracture in February 2008 during a match against Birmingham City, an incident that shocked the football world. After a lengthy rehabilitation and recovery period, Eduardo made an emotional return to the field in 2009. His ability to regain form and score again for Arsenal was an inspiration to many fans and players.

8. Leroy Sané (Manchester City, 2020)

German winger Leroy Sané suffered a severe anterior cruciate ligament injury in August 2019, sidelining him for nearly the entire 2019-2020 season. Sané worked intensively on his rehabilitation and made his competitive return before the season ended, demonstrating his determination and strength of character. Although his playing time was limited upon his return, his ability to perform at a high level after such an injury was impressive, showcasing his talent and commitment to his sport.

9. Santi Cazorla (Villarreal, 2018)

After enduring a series of severe injuries and numerous surgeries that threatened to end his career, Santi Cazorla made an incredible comeback to top-level football with Villarreal in 2018. His perseverance in overcoming these physical and mental obstacles and regaining his peak form on the pitch was acclaimed worldwide. Cazorla not only managed to play at the highest level again but also became a key player for his team, illustrating a remarkable story of resilience and passion for football.

10. Radamel Falcao (AS Monaco and Colombia, 2014-2015)

After suffering a severe knee injury that kept him out of the 2014 World Cup, Radamel Falcao experienced difficult times, including unconvincing loan spells at Manchester United and Chelsea. However, he made a triumphant return with AS Monaco, rediscovering his best form and becoming one of the top scorers in Ligue 1. His comeback also impacted the international scene, where he significantly contributed to the success of the Colombian team.

Record Attendances and Extraordinary Atmospheres

These matches, marked by record attendances and electrifying atmospheres, illustrate how fan support can become a palpable force, influencing the course of events and etching each moment into the sport's legend. Through these examples, we celebrate not only the game itself but also its unifying power, which brings individuals together in a collective experience filled with emotion and fraternity.

1. Wembley Stadium, England - 1923 FA Cup Final

The 1923 FA Cup Final at Wembley Stadium in England entered history as the first major event in what would become a legendary football venue. Attracting a staggering crowd estimated at 200,000 spectators, the match exceeded the official capacity, creating a chaotic but unforgettable atmosphere. This record attendance not only highlighted the enthusiasm for football but also marked the beginning of the Wembley Stadium era as an iconic global sports venue.

2. Celtic vs Leeds United, 1970 European Champions Cup Semi-final

The 1970 European Champions Cup semi-final match between Celtic and Leeds United set an attendance record for a European club match. The atmosphere at Hampden Park was electric, with over 136,000 fans supporting Celtic, who eventually advanced to the final, demonstrating the passion and commitment of Scottish football supporters.

3. Borussia Dortmund at Signal Iduna Park

Signal Iduna Park, particularly its south stand known as the "Yellow Wall," is renowned worldwide for its phenomenal atmosphere. Dortmund's supporters are known for their passion and unwavering support, transforming each home match into a unique and unforgettable experience, underscoring the crucial role of fans in football.

4. Galatasaray at Ali Sami Yen Stadium

The former Ali Sami Yen Stadium of Galatasaray was famous for its extraordinarily intimidating atmosphere, earning the nickname "Hell" by visiting teams. This reputation was built on the fierce and passionate support of the fans, creating a significant psychological advantage for Galatasaray during its home matches.

5. River Plate vs Boca Juniors at the Monumental

The Superclásicos between River Plate and Boca Juniors are among the most passionately contested matches in the world, but the 2018 Copa Libertadores final took a unique turn by being played in Madrid. Despite the change of venue, the atmosphere was electric, with fans from both sides bringing the intensity and passion of this iconic derby to the international stage, demonstrating the global reach and universal appeal of football.

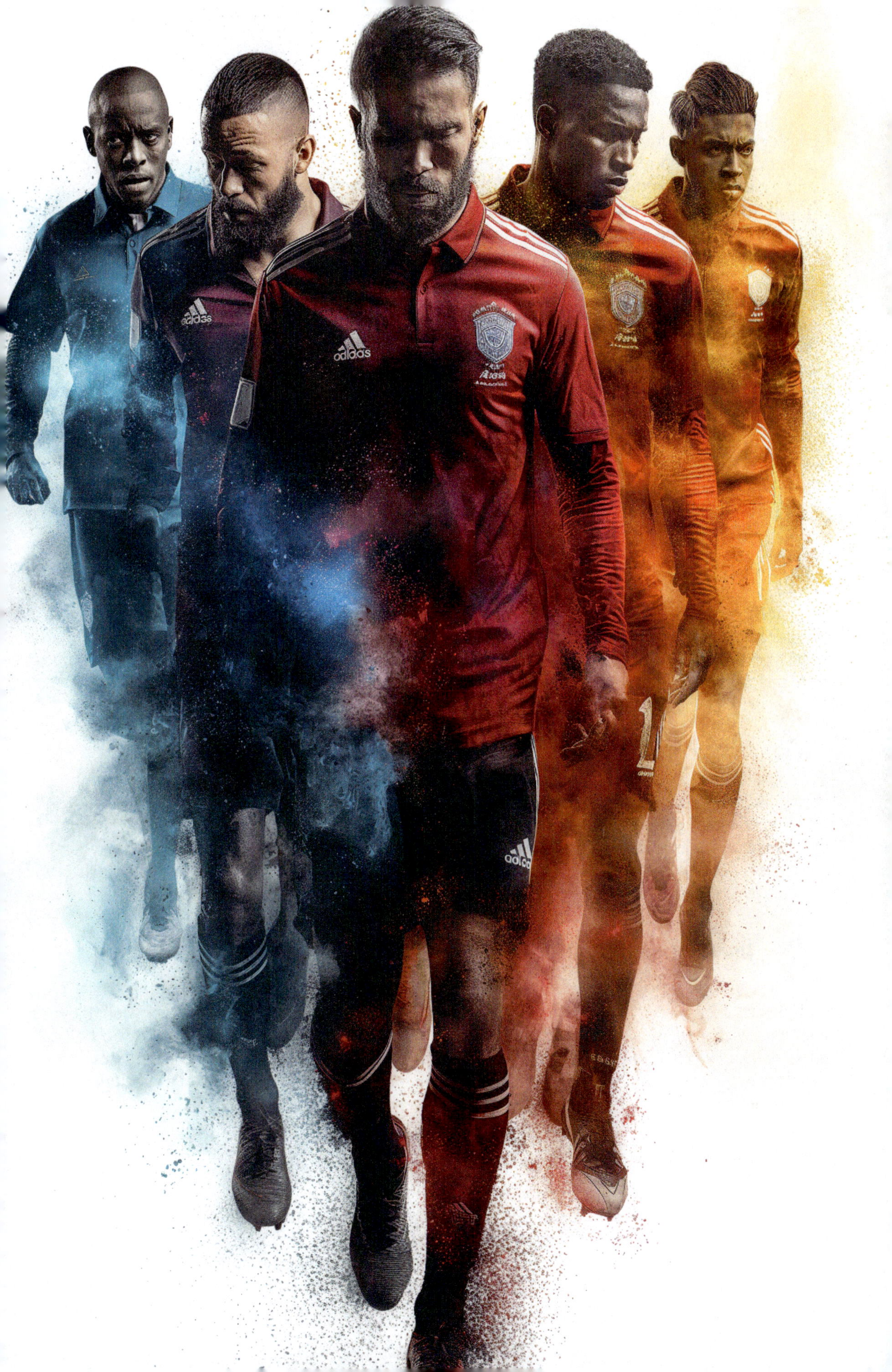
adidas

Football in Unusual Places

Explore the fascinating world of football played in extraordinary contexts and improbable locations around the globe. From zero gravity in space to floating fields in Thailand, and friendly matches in the demilitarized zone between the two Koreas, this theme highlights how football transcends conventional boundaries to adapt and thrive in surprising environments.

1. Henningsvær Stadium in Norway

Henningsvær Stadium, located on a rocky islet in the Lofoten archipelago in Norway, offers a breathtaking spectacle. Surrounded by the crystal-clear waters of the Atlantic Ocean and majestic mountains, this football field seems magically placed, occupying almost the entire surface of the islet. This unique stadium in the world, nestled in a traditional fishing village, has become a must-visit spot for travelers and football enthusiasts seeking breathtaking landscapes.

2. Football in Antarctica

In one of Earth's most hostile environments, scientists and researchers in Antarctica have embraced football as a means of recreation and mental health maintenance. Despite temperatures dropping to -50°C, football matches are organized on the ice, with participants from various nationalities, highlighting football's ability to unite people even under the most extreme conditions.

3. The River Derby (Bourton-on-the-Water, England)

Every year, the small English village of Bourton-on-the-Water hosts a unique football match in the River Windrush. Held in August, the match draws spectators from all over the region to see two local teams compete in shallow water. This picturesque tradition, existing for over 100 years, is a beautiful example of how football can become deeply ingrained in local culture and anticipated as a community event each year.

4. Underwater football (Finland)

In Finland, underwater football is a playful variant that combines diving and football. Players, equipped with fins, masks, and snorkels, compete in a pool, trying to push a weighted ball into goals at the bottom. This unusual sport requires not only swimming and diving skills but also a new tactical approach to the game, offering a completely different experience from traditional football.

5. Football in a Bolivian Prison (San Pedro, Bolivia)

San Pedro prison, unique in its kind, allows significant autonomy to its inmates, who have organized their own society. football plays a central role, serving as a pastime and a means to maintain order and discipline. Tournaments are regularly organized, reflecting the hierarchical and social structure of the prison and demonstrating how the sport can play a vital role even in the most unexpected environments.

6. Match on the Floating Field of Koh Panyee (Thailand)

The fishing village of Koh Panyee is famous for its floating football field, built by village children who wanted a place to play despite the lack of space on their rocky island. This field, anchored in the water, has inspired a generation of young players and has become a tourist attraction. It symbolizes the passion for football and the ingenuity required to overcome physical obstacles, offering inspiration for communities worldwide.

7. Blind football (Brazil and International)

Blind football, or football for the visually impaired, is played with a sound-emitting ball that allows players to locate its position by sound. Teams often consist of visually impaired players and a sighted goalkeeper. This sport has gained popularity and recognition, with international competitions such as the Paralympics. It demonstrates how football adapts to include athletes of all abilities, providing a platform for expression and equal competition.

8. Match in the Heart of the Demilitarized Zone (Korea)

A friendly football match was organized between North and South Korean soldiers in the demilitarized zone, a highly symbolic location known as one of the most militarized places on earth. Although symbolic, this match served as a gesture of goodwill between the two countries, showing how football can act as a bridge in diplomacy and peace efforts.

9. Football in the Favelas (Brazil)

Improvised football fields in Brazilian favelas are where local young talents often showcase their skills. Despite sloping fields and often precarious conditions, these football matches reflect the deep love for the sport and its central role as an escape and source of hope for many youths.

10. Football in Zero Gravity (Space)

Astronauts have played football in zero gravity aboard the International Space Station, illustrating how Earth's most popular sport can be adapted even in space. This unique match demonstrates football's universality and its ability to entertain and unite people, even under the most extreme conditions.

Success and Progress in Women's football

From resounding victories on international fields to struggles for equality off the field, along with the rise of professional leagues and the impact of inspiring icons, women's football has become a symbol of resilience, ambition, and excellence. These achievements celebrate the players, teams, and moments that have written the glorious chapters of this sport, showcasing the strength and passion that drive women's football today.

1. FIFA Women's World Cup 2019

The 2019 FIFA Women's World Cup in France was a landmark moment for women's football, drawing record audiences and filling stadiums, reflecting significant growth in interest for the sport. The United States' victory underscored their dominant position on the world stage, winning the tournament for the fourth time and highlighting the talent and competitiveness of women's football.

2. Olympique Lyonnais in the 2010s-2020s

The women's team of Olympique Lyonnais has established a dynasty in European women's football, winning multiple UEFA Champions League titles and demonstrating sustained excellence that has raised the standards of the sport. Their success has not only highlighted the club but also inspired others to invest in and value women's football.

3. Marta Vieira da Silva

Marta has transcended women's football, becoming an icon and a source of inspiration for future generations. With six FIFA World Player of the Year titles and as the all-time leading scorer in Women's World Cup history, she has broken barriers and established a legacy that will endure well beyond her playing career.

4. Pay Equality for the U.S. National Team

The U.S. women's national team has been at the forefront of the fight for pay equality, culminating in a historic agreement ensuring equal pay with the men's team. This victory marked a significant turning point in the recognition and valuation of women's football and sent a strong message about the importance of equality in sports.

5. Professionalization of Women's Leagues

The rise in professionalism of women's leagues, notably in England with the Women's Super League and in the United States with the National Women's Soccer League, has marked significant progress in women's football. These developments have provided more opportunities, greater visibility, and encouraged investment in the sport, contributing to its evolution.

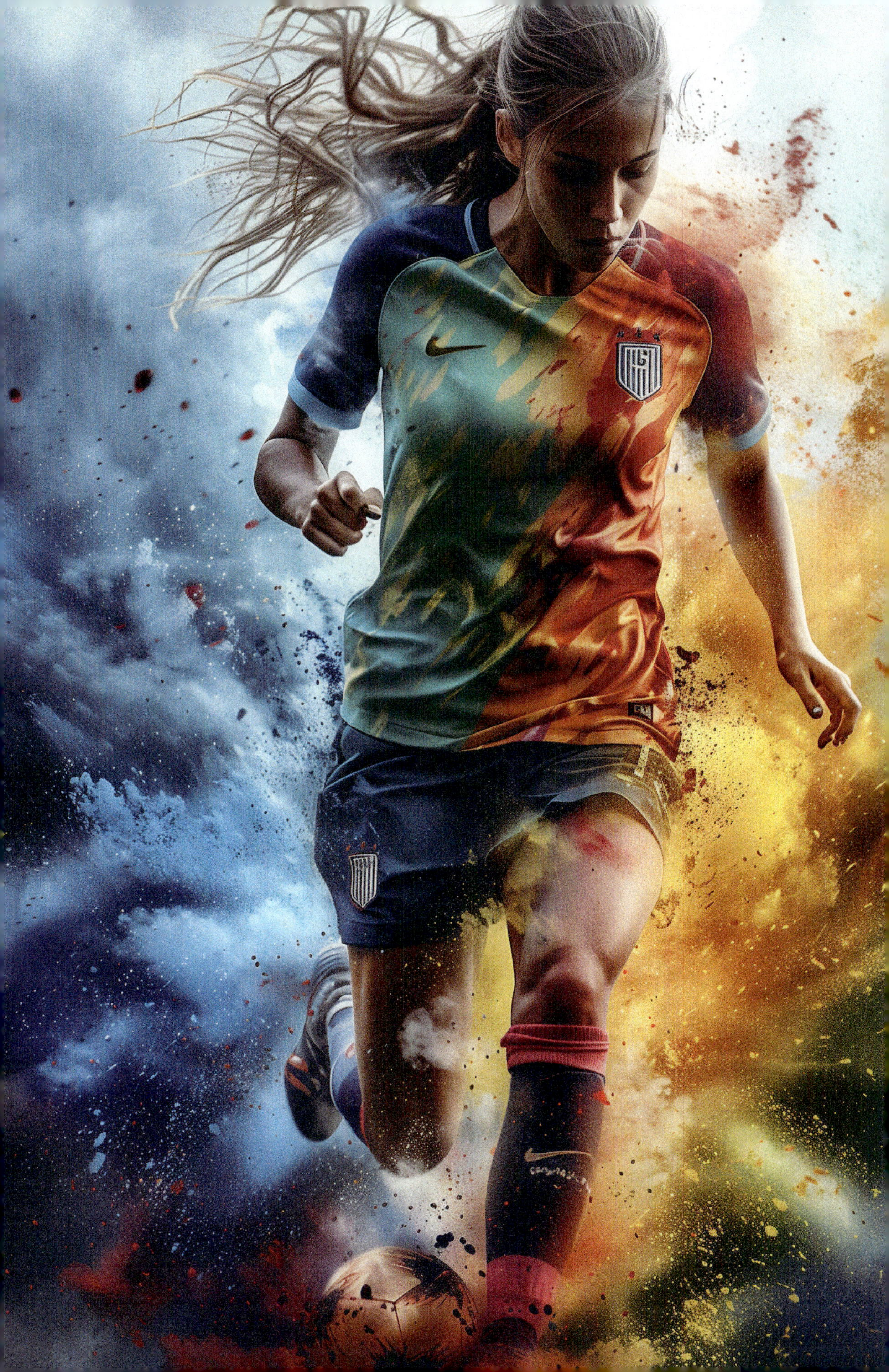

What Kind of Football Player Are You?

Explore your preferences, reactions, and skills through a series of questions to reveal the kind of football player you could be. Whether you're already playing football, are a passionate fan, or just curious to find out your alter ego on the field, this quiz is for you!

1. What is your approach during an important match?

- A. Take risks and be creative.
- B. Use my strength and speed to make a difference.
- C. Analyze and control the pace of the game.
- D. Support my teammates and be the defensive pillar.

2. What type of goal do you prefer to score?

- A. An artistic free kick.
- B. A solo run through the defense.
- C. A calculated, precise long-range strike.
- D. A powerful header from a corner.

3. How do you handle pressure?

- A. I use it to boost my creativity on the field.
- B. I focus and use my physical strength to dominate.
- C. I adopt a strategic approach to overcome challenges.
- D. I stay calm and ensure safety in defense.

4. What is your ideal role in a team?

- A. The playmaker who creates opportunities.
- B. The star striker who consistently scores.
- C. The strategic midfielder who controls the game.
- D. The solid defender who can always be relied upon.

5. How do you react to a loss?

- A. I think about how I can be more creative next time.
- B. I work even harder physically for the next time.
- C. I analyze the game to understand what didn't work.
- D. I motivate the team to stay united and improve.

6. What is your most important asset?

A. My game vision and creativity.

B. My speed and power.

C. My ability to read the game and make decisive passes.

D. My solidity in defense and my leadership.

7. In a tough situation during a match, what would be your reaction?

A. Innovate creatively to overcome obstacles.

B. Take the initiative to turn the situation around with your strength.

C. Analyze and orchestrate the game to find strategic solutions.

D. Solidify the defense, becoming the pillar your team can rely on.

8. What motivates you to play football?

A. Expressing my creativity and talent.

B. Passion for the game and the desire to win.

C. Love for strategy and competition.

D. The feeling of belonging to a team.

9. How do you train?

A. I focus on improving my technical skills.

B. I prioritize physical training to increase my strength and speed.

C. I study the game to improve my tactical understanding.

D. I work on my resilience and defensive coordination.

10. Who is your role model in the world of football?

A. A player known for their technique and creativity.

B. A legendary scorer known for their power.

C. A midfielder renowned for their game intelligence.

D. A defender famous for their solidity and leadership.

Mostly A's: You are an artist on the field, reminiscent of Lionel Messi. Your creativity and technical finesse define you.

Mostly B's: You are a force of nature, like Cristiano Ronaldo. Your power and scoring ability are unmatched.

Mostly C's: You are the brain of the team, in the style of Xavi Hernandez. Your vision and tactical intelligence lead the game.

Mostly D's: You are the defensive rock, similar to Sergio Ramos. Your strength and leadership in defense are crucial for your team.

QUIZ

1. Which team won the FIFA World Cup in 2014?

A. Brazil

B. Germany

C. Argentina

2. Who scored the "Goal of the Century" at the FIFA World Cup in 1986?

A. Diego Maradona

B. Pelé

C. Zinedine Zidane

3. What is the standard distance from the penalty spot to the goal?

A. 9.15 meters

B. 10.97 meters

C. 11 meters

4. Which player holds the record for the most goals in FIFA World Cup history?

A. Miroslav Klose

B. Ronaldo Nazário

C. Just Fontaine

5. Which country invented modern football?

A. Germany

B. England

C. Italy

6. Which team is nicknamed "The Azzurri"?

A. France

B. Brazil

C. Italy

7. Who won the Ballon d'Or in 2001?

A. Zinedine Zidane

B. Luis Figo

C. Michael Owen

8. What is the largest football stadium in the world in terms of capacity?

A. Maracanã

B. Camp Nou

C. Rungrado 1st of May

9. How many players are there on the field for a football team during an official match (excluding the goalkeeper)?

A. 10

B. 11

C. 12

10. Which team has won the most UEFA Champions League titles?

A. FC Barcelona

B. Real Madrid

C. AC Milan

11. In what year was the offside rule introduced in football?

A. 1863

B. 1925

C. 1907

12. Which player is known for executing a "Panenka" during a penalty in the Euro 1976 final?

A. Zinedine Zidane

B. Antonín Panenka

C. Andrea Pirlo

13. Which country hosted the FIFA World Cup in 2010?

A. Germany

B. South Africa

C. Brazil

14. Who is the only player to have won three FIFA World Cups?

A. Pelé

B. Diego Maradona

C. Ronaldo Nazário

15. What is the name of the trophy awarded to the winner of the FIFA World Cup?

A. Jules Rimet Trophy

B. FIFA Trophy

C. FIFA World Cup Trophy

16. Which football team is nicknamed "The Reds"?

A. Manchester United

B. Arsenal

C. Liverpool

17. Who invented the "Total Football" tactic?

A. Johan Cruyff

B. Rinus Michels

C. Pep Guardiola

18. What is the record for the most expensive football transfer in history?

A. Neymar Jr.

B. Kylian Mbappé

C. Cristiano Ronaldo

19. What is the name given to the derby between Real Madrid and FC Barcelona?

A. El Clásico

B. Derby della Madonnina

C. Le Classique

20. Who is the player with the most Ballon d'Or awards?

A. Lionel Messi

B. Cristiano Ronaldo

C. Michel Platini

21. Which English club is known by the nickname "The Gunners"?

A. Chelsea

B. Arsenal

C. Manchester City

22. Who was the first player to receive the Ballon d'Or?

A. Alfredo Di Stefano

B. Stanley Matthews

C. Johan Cruyff

23. In which country did the FIFA World Cup 2022 take place?

A. Qatar

B. United States

C. Australia

24. Who is the all-time top scorer in the UEFA Champions League?

A. Lionel Messi

B. Cristiano Ronaldo

C. Raúl González

25. Which nation won Euro 2016?

A. France

B. Germany

C. Portugal

26. What is the nickname of the Argentine national team?

A. Los Cafeteros

B. La Roja

C. La Albiceleste

27. Which country won the first FIFA Women's World Cup in 1991?

A. United States

B. Germany

C. Norway

28. Who scored the winning goal in the FIFA World Cup 2010 final?

A. Andrés Iniesta

B. David Villa

C. Xavi Hernández

29. Which football team is nicknamed "La Celeste"?

A. Uruguay

B. Italy

C. France

30. Who invented the famous "body feint" in football?

A. Johan Cruyff

B. Pelé

C. Garrincha

31. Which team went undefeated throughout the Premier League 2003-2004 season?

A. Chelsea

B. Manchester United

C. Arsenal

32. Which player has won the most FIFA World Cups?

A. Pelé

B. Maradona

C. Zidane

33. What is the nationality of coach José Mourinho?

A. Spanish

B. Portuguese

C. Italian

34. Which team won the first FIFA World Cup in 1930?

A. Brazil

B. Argentina

C. Uruguay

35. Which team achieved the "Treble," winning the Champions League, the national league, and the national cup in the same season for the first time?

A. FC Barcelona

B. Manchester United

C. Bayern Munich

Answers

1. B. Germany	of May	Cup Trophy	23. A. Qatar	30. C. Garrincha
2. A. Diego Maradona	9. A. 10	16. C. Liverpool	24. B. Cristiano Ronaldo	31. C. Arsenal
3. C. 11 meters	10. B. Real Madrid	17. B. Rinus Michels	25. C. Portugal	32. A. Pelé
4. A. Miroslav Klose	11. B. 1925	18. A. Neymar Jr.	26. C. La Albiceleste	33. B. Portuguese
5. B. England	12. B. Antonín Panenka	19. A. El Clásico	27. A. United States	34. C. Uruguay
6. C. Italy	13. B. South Africa	20. A. Lionel Messi	28. A. Andrés Iniesta	35. B. Manchester United
7. C. Michael Owen	14. A. Pelé	21. B. Arsenal		
8. C. Rungrado 1st	15. C. FIFA World	22. B. Stanley Matthews	29. A. Uruguay	

QUIZ

1. Which player has won the most UEFA Champions League titles?

A. Cristiano Ronaldo

B. Lionel Messi

C. Francisco Gento

2. Which national team is nicknamed "La Roja"?

A. Chile

B. Spain

C. Mexico

3. Who scored the fastest goal in a FIFA World Cup final?

A. Pelé

B. Johan Cruyff

C. Zinedine Zidane

4. Who is the only player to have been sent off in a FIFA World Cup final?

A. Zinedine Zidane

B. Marcel Desailly

C. Giancarlo Antognoni

5. Which country has the most Copa America wins?

A. Brazil

B. Argentina

C. Uruguay

6. Who was the first footballer to win the new format of the Ballon d'Or in 2010?

A. Lionel Messi

B. Cristiano Ronaldo

C. Andrés Iniesta

7. Which city hosted the finals of the FIFA World Cup and UEFA Champions League in the same year?

A. Madrid

B. London

C. Berlin

8. Who is the all-time top scorer of the Premier League?

A. Alan Shearer

B. Wayne Rooney

C. Thierry Henry

9. Which club holds the record for the most consecutive wins in the top five European leagues?

A. Juventus

B. Bayern Munich

C. Manchester City

10. Which was the first non-European club to win the FIFA Club World Cup?

A. Boca Juniors

B. Corinthians

C. Al-Ahly

11. Who invented the "Marseille turn" or "roulette" dribble?

A. Diego Maradona

B. Zinedine Zidane

C. Pelé

12. Which team holds the record for the most goals scored in a single Premier League season?

A. Manchester City

B. Liverpool

C. Chelsea

13. Who is the oldest player to have participated in a FIFA World Cup?

A. Roger Milla

B. Peter Shilton

C. Essam El-Hadary

14. Which team won the first edition of the Euro in 1960?

A. USSR

B. Yugoslavia

C. France

15. Which player holds the record for the most international caps?

A. Cristiano Ronaldo

B. Ahmed Hassan

C. Soh Chin Ann

16. Who scored the most goals in a single Bundesliga season?

A. Gerd Müller

B. Robert Lewandowski

C. Pierre-Emerick Aubameyang

17. Which player has scored in four different World Cups?

A. Cristiano Ronaldo

B. Pelé

C. Miroslav Klose

18. Which football team won their first international match by the largest margin?

A. Australia

B. Hungary

C. England

19. Who is the youngest captain to have won the FIFA World Cup?

A. Bobby Moore

B. Diego Maradona

C. Pelé

20. Which is the only national team to have participated in every FIFA World Cup?

A. Brazil

B. Germany

C. Italy

21. What is the record for the highest attendance at a football match?

A. 199,854
B. 120,000
C. 99,354

22. Which football club was the first to achieve a sextuple (winning six trophies in a single season)?

A. FC Barcelona
B. Manchester United
C. Bayern Munich

23. What is the oldest football stadium still in use in the world?

A. Anfield
B. Stamford Bridge
C. Bramall Lane

24. Who scored the most goals in a single edition of the Euros?

A. Michel Platini
B. Cristiano Ronaldo
C. Antoine Griezmann

25. Which team has won the most Serie A titles?

A. AC Milan
B. Inter Milan
C. Juventus

26. Who is the player with the most goals in a single Ligue 1 season?

A. Zlatan Ibrahimović
B. Kylian Mbappé
C. Josip Skoblar

27. Which team has won the most consecutive titles in one of the top five European leagues?

A. Bayern Munich
B. Juventus
C. Real Madrid

28. Who is the player with the most red cards in Premier League history?

A. Roy Keane
B. Patrick Vieira
C. Duncan Ferguson

29. Which player has won the most UEFA Champions League titles as captain?

A. Franz Beckenbauer
B. Carles Puyol
C. Paolo Maldini

30. Who is the player with the most assists in the history of the UEFA Champions League?

A. Lionel Messi
B. Cristiano Ronaldo
C. Ryan Giggs

31. Which national team has the longest consecutive winning streak in official matches?

A. Spain
B. Brazil
C. Italy

32. Which team has won the most consecutive matches across all competitions?

A. Real Madrid
B. Bayern Munich
C. Corinthians

33. What is the nationality of coach José Mourinho?

A. Spanish
B. Portuguese
C. Italian

34. Which team won the first FIFA World Cup in 1930?

A. Brazil
B. Argentina
C. Uruguay

35. What is the world record for the most goals scored by a national football team in a single FIFA-recognized international match?

A. Australia with 31 goals
B. Hungary with 10 goals
C. Kuwait with 20 goals

Answers

1. C. Francisco Gento	8. A. Alan Shearer	15. C. Soh Chin Ann	22. A. FC Barcelona	29. C. Paolo Maldini
2. B. Spain	9. C. Manchester City	16. B. Robert Lewandowski	23. C. Bramall Lane	30. A. Lionel Messi
3. A. Pelé	10. B. Corinthians	17. C. Miroslav Klose	24. A. Michel Platini	31. A. Spain
4. A. Zinedine Zidane	11. B. Zinedine Zidane	18. A. Australia	25. C. Juventus	32. B. Bayern Munich
5. C. Uruguay	12. A. Manchester City	19. C. Pelé	26. C. Josip Skoblar	33. B. Portuguese
6. A. Lionel Messi	13. C. Essam El-Hadary	20. A. Brazil	27. B. Juventus	34. C. Uruguay
7. B. London	14. A. USSR	21. A. 199,854	28. C. Duncan Ferguson	35. A. Australia

Introduction to Euro 2024

General Overview of Euro 2024

The 2024 UEFA European Football Championship, commonly referred to as Euro 2024, will be the 17th edition of this prestigious competition organized by UEFA. This quadrennial event will gather Europe's top national teams to determine the continent's champion. Euro 2024 is set to take place in Germany, giving this football-passionate country the opportunity to host the tournament for the second time, following the 1988 edition.

The tournament will run from June 14 to July 14, 2024, featuring a total of 51 matches played across 10 stadiums in 10 German cities. Twenty-four teams will participate in the final stage, aiming to succeed Portugal, the previous winners in 2021. Teams will be divided into six groups of four, with the top two from each group and the four best third-placed teams advancing to the round of 16.

Euro 2024 promises to be a high-level football spectacle, showcasing some of the world's best players. Fans globally are eagerly anticipating watching their favorite teams compete for the European champion title. Germany's stadiums, known for their modern architecture and electric atmosphere, will provide an ideal setting for this major sporting event..

Significance of the Euro in Football

The European Football Championship is regarded as the second most prestigious international football competition after the FIFA World Cup. The Euro brings together the top football nations from Europe, a continent that traditionally dominates global football. Winning the Euro is a significant achievement for any national team, proving its supremacy on the European stage.

Beyond the sporting aspect, the Euro also holds substantial cultural and social importance. It unites millions of fans across Europe and the world, fostering a sense of unity and camaraderie around the passion for football. Euro matches are celebratory and festive occasions, transcending borders and differences.

Economically, hosting the Euro generates significant benefits for the host country. Investments in infrastructure, tourism, and event-related spending boost the local economy and create jobs. The Euro also serves as an exceptional showcase for the host nation, attracting global attention and enhancing its international image.

In summary, Euro 2024 is set to be a major football event with significant sporting, cultural, social, and economic stakes. Its importance in the football world makes it a must-watch event for players, teams, and fans worldwide.

History of the Euro

Review of Previous Editions

The European Football Championship, commonly known as the Euro, has a rich and exciting history since its inception in 1960. The first edition, held in France, featured only four teams in the final stage: USSR, Yugoslavia, Czechoslovakia, and France. The Soviet Union won this first European title.

Over the years, the competition has expanded and gained prestige. The number of teams in the final stage has increased from 4 in 1960 to 8 in 1980, 16 in 1996, and finally 24 since 2016. Nations such as Germany (1972, 1980, 1996), Spain (1964, 2008, 2012), and France (1984, 2000) have won the tournament multiple times.

The Euro has been the stage for legendary matches and moments. Notable are the 1960 semi-final between France and Yugoslavia ending 4-5, Czechoslovakia's 1976 title after a penalty shootout against Germany, Denmark's surprise victory in 1992, and Greece's unexpected triumph in 2004.

Memorable Moments and Historic Records

Each edition of the Euro has delivered strong performances and individual feats that have made history. Iconic moments include Marco Van Basten's winning goal in the 1988 final, Peter Schmeichel's decisive save in the 1992 penalty shootout, David Trezeguet's golden goal in the 2000 final, and Michel Platini's hat-trick against Yugoslavia in 1984.

The Euro also allows players to set records. Cristiano Ronaldo is the top scorer in Euro history with 14 goals, holds the record for most games played (25), and has participated in the most finals (5). Michel Platini scored 9 goals at Euro 1984, a record for a single edition.

The competition also boasts team records such as the most goals scored in one edition by France in 1984 (14 goals) and the widest victory of Spain over Slovakia in 2020 (5-0).

Germany as Host Country

Presentation of Germany as Host

Germany was chosen to host Euro 2024 by UEFA's Executive Committee on September 27, 2018. This will be the second time the country hosts this competition, following the 1988 edition held in West Germany. Germany boasts a rich football tradition and proven experience in organizing major sports events.

Centrally located in Europe, Germany offers quality infrastructure and an extensive transport network, making it easy for teams and fans to travel. Known for its hospitality and football enthusiasm, Germany ensures a festive atmosphere throughout the competition.

Germany is a football nation with one of the most successful national teams globally (4 World Cups and 3 Euros) and internationally renowned clubs like Bayern Munich and Borussia Dortmund. Football is an integral part of German culture, arousing immense passion nationwide.

Cities and Stadiums Selected for Euro 2024

Euro 2024 will take place in 10 stadiums across 10 German cities. These modern and functional venues will provide optimal playing conditions and a unique experience for spectators. Here are the cities and stadiums selected:

Berlin - Olympiastadion (capacity: 74,475)

Munich - Allianz Arena (75,024)

Dortmund - Signal Iduna Park (66,099)

Gelsenkirchen - Veltins-Arena (54,740)

Stuttgart - Mercedes-Benz Arena (54,697)

Hamburg - Volksparkstadion (51,500)

Düsseldorf - Merkur Spiel-Arena (51,031)

Cologne - RheinEnergieStadion (49,827)

Leipzig - Red Bull Arena (49,539)

Frankfurt - Deutsche Bank Park (48,387)

Qualified Teams

Qualification Process for Euro 2024

Les 24 équipes qualifiées pour l'Euro 2024

After an exciting qualifying phase and suspenseful playoffs, the 24 nations that will participate in Euro 2024 in Germany from June 14 to July 14 are now confirmed. Here's an overview of the teams involved.

The 21 Direct Qualifiers

By the end of the qualifiers from March to November 2023, 21 teams had already secured their tickets to Germany: Germany (host nation), England, Austria, Belgium, Croatia, Denmark, Scotland, Spain, France, Hungary, Italy, Netherlands, Portugal, Czech Republic, Romania, Serbia, Slovakia, Slovenia, Switzerland, and Turkey. This lineup includes usual powerhouses such as France, Spain, England, Italy, Belgium, and Portugal, as well as some surprises like Hungary and Romania.

The 3 Playoff Teams

The last three tickets were awarded through a 12-team playoff held on March 21 and 26, 2024. Poland, Ukraine, and Georgia, in its first participation, secured the final qualifying spots.

Composition of the 6 Groups

The draw held on December 2, 2023, in Hamburg distributed the 24 qualifiers into 6 groups of four: Group A (Germany, Scotland, Hungary, Switzerland), Group B (Spain, Croatia, Italy, Albania), Group C (Slovenia, Denmark, Serbia, England), Group D (Poland, Netherlands, Austria, France), Group E (Belgium, Slovakia, Romania, Ukraine), Group F (Turkey, Georgia, Portugal, Czech Republic). While most favorites were placed in manageable groups, Group B with Spain, Croatia, and Italy, and Group D with France, Netherlands, and Poland appear particularly challenging.

The group stage will begin on June 14 with the opening match between Germany and Scotland in Munich and will conclude on June 26. The top two teams from each group and the four best third-placed teams will advance to the round of 16. After 51 matches, the final is scheduled for July 14 in Berlin. Football fans have already marked the dates: Euro 2024 is set to be the must-watch football event of the summer!

Players to Watch

Stars of the Tournament

Euro 2024 will be an opportunity to see Europe's greatest football stars shine. Established international players are expected to lead their teams towards the title. Among them, Kylian Mbappé, the French forward and 2018 World Cup champion with multiple titles at Paris Saint-Germain, will be one of the main attractions. His speed, skill, and goal-scoring ability make him a spectacular and decisive player.

From England, Harry Kane, the top scorer of the 2018 World Cup and captain of the national team, will try to lead the Three Lions to their first European title. His scoring efficiency and leadership will be crucial. Kevin De Bruyne, the playmaker for Belgium and Manchester City, is also highly anticipated. His game vision, passing quality, and scoring ability make him one of the most complete midfielders in the world.

Other stars like Cristiano Ronaldo (Portugal), Robert Lewandowski (Poland), Luka Modric (Croatia), and Joshua Kimmich (Germany) will also be in the spotlight. Their experience and talent will be essential to guide their respective teams to success.

Emerging Talents to Follow

Beyond the established stars, Euro 2024 could reveal new talents to the broader public. Young promising players will have the chance to make a name for themselves on the international stage. Among them, Jamal Musiala, the German attacking midfielder from Bayern Munich, already impresses with his maturity and creativity despite his young age. He could be one of the revelations of the tournament.

Pedri, the Spanish midfielder from FC Barcelona, is another bright prospect of European football. His technical skill, game vision, and ability to escape pressing make him a rare talent. With Spain, he aims to follow in the footsteps of his illustrious predecessors.

From England, Phil Foden (Manchester City) and Bukayo Saka (Arsenal) represent the new generation of the Three Lions. Their speed, dribbling, and attacking threat consistently pose a danger to opposing defenses. They could symbolize a conquering England.

Other young talents like Eduardo Camavinga (France), Gavi (Spain), Florian Wirtz (Germany), and Ryan Gravenberch (Netherlands) will also have a role to play. Euro 2024 could be the tournament that showcases their abilities to a global audience.

Technology and Innovation

Use of Technology in Euro 2024

Euro 2024 will showcase the latest technological advancements in the field of football. These innovations aim to enhance the experience for players, referees, and spectators, while ensuring fairness and integrity of the game.

Video Assistant Referee (VAR), already utilized during Euro 2021, will be deployed again in 2024. This system allows referees to review and correct controversial decisions related to goals, penalties, direct red cards, and identity mistakes. VAR has proven its usefulness in reducing refereeing errors and making the game fairer.

Goal-line technology, which accurately determines whether the ball has fully crossed the goal line, will also be used. This system, consisting of high-precision cameras and sensors in the ball, sends a signal to the referee's watch in case of a goal. This technology has ended controversies over ghost goals.

Expected Innovations and Their Impact on the Game

Beyond these proven technologies, Euro 2024 could be a testing ground for new innovations. Real-time player and ball tracking systems could be used to collect precise tactical and physical data. This information would allow coaches to finely analyze their team's performance and adapt their strategy accordingly.

Artificial intelligence might also make its debut to assist in referees' decision-making. Real-time video analysis algorithms could automatically detect fouls, offsides, or handballs in the box, and alert the officials. This technology, still in development, could eventually relieve referees from some of the pressure and make the game smoother.

For spectators, innovations are expected to enrich their experience. Dedicated mobile apps could offer replays, live statistics, exclusive camera angles, and player information. Augmented reality experiences could allow fans to visualize tactical data overlaid on the field, for an even greater immersion.

Finally, technological innovations could be employed for sustainability and environmental purposes. Intelligent systems for managing energy and water in stadiums, low-carbon transportation solutions for fans, or jerseys made from recycled materials are all avenues to make Euro 2024 an eco-responsible event.

Strategies and Tactics

Team Strategy Analysis

Euro 2024 will see the top European nations clash, each with its own playing identity and strategy aiming to win the title. Coaches will face the challenging task of implementing coherent and effective game systems that play to their squad's strengths while accounting for their opponents.

Teams like Spain and Germany are renowned for their possession-based play, focusing on quick and accurate ball movement. Their aim is to monopolize the ball, wear down the opponent, and create scoring opportunities through tight passing combinations. This strategy requires technically skilled players who can make smart decisions under pressure.

Other nations, like England or Portugal, prefer a more direct and vertical approach, relying on the speed and power of their forwards. Their strategy is to recover the ball quickly and launch counter-attacks to outpace the opposing defense. This approach demands midfielders who can swiftly deliver the ball and forwards who are efficient and accurate in front of the goal.

More defensively oriented teams, such as Italy or Croatia, rely on rigorous tactical organization to neutralize opposition attacks. Their priority is to protect their goal by defending as a unit and then counter-attacking at opportune moments. This strategy requires great collective discipline and effective management of effort.

Key Tactics That Could Define Euro 2024

Beyond overall strategies, specific tactics could prove decisive at Euro 2024. High pressing, involving intense pressure on the opponent's ball carrier immediately after losing possession, will likely be key. This tactic allows teams to quickly regain possession in the opponent's half and create scoring opportunities, though it requires significant energy and perfect coordination among players.

The use of full-backs as offensive weapons will also be scrutinized. Many teams rely on their full-backs' forward runs to create numerical advantages and deliver crosses from the touchline. This tactic is particularly effective against teams that congest the middle, but it can leave spaces behind the defense if the ball is lost.

Set-piece management, often decisive in major tournaments, will be another focal point. Teams will practice elaborate routines on corners and free-kicks to confuse defenses. Player blocks, screens, and staggered runs are tactics used to create confusion and break free from markers.

Lastly, the use of substitutes as a tactical asset will be crucial. With the ability to make five substitutions per match, coaches can significantly alter their team's setup during the game. Introducing fresh players with different profiles can change the course of the match in the final minutes.

Records and Statistics

Historical Euro Records

Since its inception in 1960, the Euro has seen numerous records set over the editions. These records highlight the rich history of the competition and the exceptional performances by participating nations and players.

Collectively, Germany and Spain hold the record for the most final victories, with three titles each. Germany won in 1972, 1980, and 1996, while Spain triumphed in 1964, 2008, and 2012. These nations have shaped Euro history with their consistency at the highest level and their ability to secure titles across generations.

The largest victory in a Euro match belongs to the Netherlands, who defeated Yugoslavia 6-1 during the 2000 edition. This match remains one of the most dominant displays in tournament history.

Individually, Michel Platini and Cristiano Ronaldo share the record for most goals scored in the final phases of the Euro, with 9 goals each. The Frenchman achieved this feat in just one edition, in 1984, while the Portuguese spread his goals across five participations, from 2004 to 2021. These outstanding forwards have left their mark on the Euro with their scoring prowess and efficiency.

Cristiano Ronaldo also holds the record for the most matches played in the final stages of the Euro, with 25 appearances, ahead of Bastian Schweinsteiger and Gianluigi Buffon, who each have 18 appearances. Ronaldo's remarkable longevity highlights his ability to maintain top-level performance over an extended period.

Potential Records to Break in 2024

Euro 2024 provides teams and players a unique opportunity to make competition history in Germany, setting or equaling records. This tournament is a perfect stage for new legendary performances and pushing the limits of football achievements.

Collectively, Spain could become the most titled nation in Euro history with a victory in 2024. A win would make Spain the record holder with four championships, confirming Spanish dominance in European football in the 21st century.

Individually, Cristiano Ronaldo, if selected by Portugal, could improve his own scoring record in the finals. With 9 goals, he is currently tied with Michel Platini. Just one more goal would make him the outright top scorer in Euro history. He could also extend his record for the most matches played and participations in the competition.

Young players like Kylian Mbappé (France) or Erling Haaland (Norway), if they live up to their immense potential, might also challenge records for early career achievements. Mbappé, who scored in 2021 at 19, could become the youngest player to reach five goals in the final stages of the Euro.

Anecdotes

Interesting and Surprising Anecdotes

Beyond these moments of glory, the Euro has also been the stage for more unusual anecdotes that have contributed to the competition's rich history. Did you know that the Henri Delaunay Trophy, awarded to the Euro winner, was stolen twice? First in 1966, only to be found by a dog named Pickles in a London bush. Then again in 1983, before being recovered wrapped in a trash bag.

In Euro 1992, the Danish team was added at the last moment to replace Yugoslavia, which was excluded due to war. The Danish players, most of whom were on vacation, had to return urgently to compete in the tournament. Against all odds, this team won the Euro, achieving one of the most improbable feats in football history.

In 2004, Greece created another sensation by winning the Euro while not being considered a major footballing nation. The Greeks eliminated the reigning champions, France, in the quarterfinals before triumphing over Portugal in the final in Lisbon's stadium.

Euro 2024 Predictions

Experience the thrill of Euro 2024 with our predictions calendar designed for football enthusiasts! As the best European teams prepare to face off on German soil, our calendar offers the unique opportunity to follow each match, analyze performances, and make your own predictions.

Group A

1 — Munich, ven, 14/06/2024, 21:00 — Germany vs Scotland
2 — Cologne, sam, 15/06/2024, 15:00 — Hungary vs Switzerland
14 — Stuttgart, mer, 19/06/2024, 18:00 — Germany vs Hungary
13 — Cologne, mer, 19/06/2024, 21:00 — Scotland vs Switzerland
25 — Frankfurt, dim, 23/06/2024, 21:00 — Switzerland vs Germany
26 — Stuttgart, dim, 23/06/2024, 21:00 — Scotland vs Hungary

Group B

3 — Berlin, sam, 15/06/2024, 18:00 — Spain vs Croatia
4 — Dortmund, sam, 15/06/2024, 21:00 — Italy vs Albania
15 — Hamburg, mer, 19/06/2024, 15:00 — Croatia vs Albania
16 — Gelsenkirchen, jeu, 20/06/2024, 21:00 — Spain vs Italy
27 — Dusseldorf, lun, 24/06/2024, 21:00 — Albania vs Spain
28 — Leipzig, lun, 24/06/2024, 21:00 — Croatia vs Italy

Group C

6 — Stuttgart, dim, 16/06/2024, 18:00 — Slovenia vs Denmark
5 — Gelsenkirchen, dim, 16/06/2024, 21:00 — Serbia vs England
18 — Munich, jeu, 20/06/2024, 15:00 — Slovenia vs Serbia
17 — Frankfurt, jeu, 20/06/2024, 18:00 — Denmark vs England
29 — Cologne, mar, 25/06/2024, 21:00 — England vs Slovenia
30 — Munich, mar, 25/06/2024, 21:00 — Denmark vs Serbia

Group D

7 — Hamburg, dim, 16/06/2024, 15:00 — Poland vs Netherlands
8 — Dusseldorf, lun, 17/06/2024, 21:00 — Austria vs France
19 — Berlin, ven, 21/06/2024, 18:00 — Poland vs Austria
20 — Leipzig, ven, 21/06/2024, 21:00 — Netherlands vs France
31 — Berlin, mar, 25/06/2024, 18:00 — Netherlands vs Austria
32 — Dortmund, mar, 25/06/2024, 18:00 — France vs Poland

Group E

10 — Munich, lun, 17/06/2024, 15:00 — Romania vs Ukraine
9 — Frankfurt, lun, 17/06/2024, 18:00 — Belgium vs Slovakia
21 — Dusseldorf, ven, 21/06/2024, 15:00 — Slovakia vs Ukraine
22 — Cologne, sam, 22/06/2024, 21:00 — Belgium vs Romania
33 — Frankfurt, mer, 26/06/2024, 18:00 — Slovakia vs Romania
34 — Stuttgart, mer, 26/06/2024, 18:00 — Ukraine vs Belgium

Group F

11 — Dortmund, mar, 18/06/2024, 18:00 — Türkiye vs Georgia
12 — Leipzig, mar, 18/06/2024, 21:00 — Portugal vs Czechia
24 — Hamburg, sam, 22/06/2024, 15:00 — Georgia vs Czechia
23 — Dortmund, sam, 22/06/2024, 18:00 — Türkiye vs Portugal
35 — Gelsenkirchen, mer, 26/06/2024, 21:00 — Georgia vs Portugal
36 — Hamburg, mer, 26/06/2024, 21:00 — Czechia vs Türkiye

Round of 16

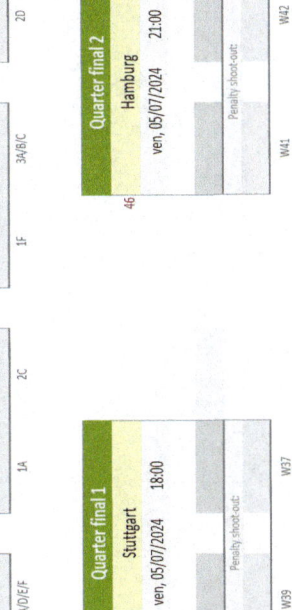

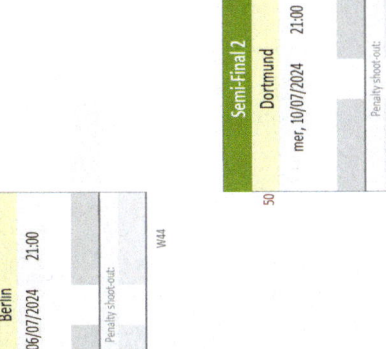

Round of 16 - 1 — Berlin — sam, 29/06/2024 — 18:00
38 — 2A vs 2B — Penalty shoot-out:

Round of 16 - 2 — Dortmund — sam, 29/06/2024 — 21:00
37 — 1A vs 2C — Penalty shoot-out:

Round of 16 - 3 — Gelsenkirchen — dim, 30/06/2024 — 18:00
40 — 1C vs 3D/E/F — Penalty shoot-out:

Round of 16 - 4 — Cologne — dim, 30/06/2024 — 21:00
39 — 1B vs 3A/D/E/F — Penalty shoot-out:

Round of 16 - 5 — Dusseldorf — lun, 01/07/2024 — 18:00
42 — 2D vs 2E — Penalty shoot-out:

Round of 16 - 6 — Frankfurt — lun, 01/07/2024 — 21:00
41 — 1F vs 3A/B/C — Penalty shoot-out:

Round of 16 - 7 — Munich — mar, 02/07/2024 — 18:00
43 — 1E vs 3A/B/C/D — Penalty shoot-out:

Round of 16 - 8 — Leipzig — mar, 02/07/2024 — 21:00
44 — 1D vs 2F — Penalty shoot-out:

Quarter finals

Quarter final 1 — Stuttgart — ven, 05/07/2024 — 18:00
45 — W39 vs W37 — Penalty shoot-out:

Quarter final 2 — Hamburg — ven, 05/07/2024 — 21:00
46 — W41 vs W42 — Penalty shoot-out:

Quarter final 3 — Dusseldorf — sam, 06/07/2024 — 18:00
48 — W40 vs W38 — Penalty shoot-out:

Quarter final 4 — Berlin — sam, 06/07/2024 — 21:00
47 — W43 vs W44 — Penalty shoot-out:

Semi-Finals

Semi-Final 1 — Munich — mar, 09/07/2024 — 21:00
49 — W45 vs W46 — Penalty shoot-out:

Semi-Final 2 — Dortmund — mer, 10/07/2024 — 21:00
50 — W47 vs W48 — Penalty shoot-out:

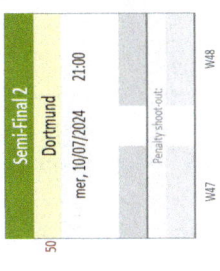

Final

Final — Berlin — dim, 14/07/2024 — 21:00
51 — Penalty shoot-out:

European Champion 2024:

97

Scan this QR code to discover videos of the most memorable actions mentioned in this book. Enjoy these football highlights!

Thank you for reading this book! If you enjoyed it, we would be delighted if you took a moment to leave a review. Your feedback is valuable and helps inspire future creations.

Printed in Great Britain
by Amazon